THE MISER
THE IDIOT

Molière
THE MISER
THE IDIOT
new versions by
Ranjit Bolt

OBERON BOOKS
LONDON

First published in 2001 by Oberon Books Ltd
521 Caledonian Road, London N7 9RH
Tel: +44 (0) 20 7607 3637 / Fax: +44 (0) 20 7607 3629
e-mail: info@oberonbooks.com
www.oberonbooks.com

A catalogue record for this book is available from the British Library.

PB ISBN: 9781840022162
E ISBN: 9781783192540

Cover design by Andrzej Klimowski

Visit www.oberonbooks.com to read more about all our books and to buy them. You will also find features, author interviews and news of any author events, and you can sign up for e-newsletters and be the first to hear about our new releases.

Printed on FSC® accredited paper

Contents

INTRODUCTION

Ranjit Bolt

I have always thought that satirical plays, if they are good, ought in theory, and probably in practise also, to benefit from updating. There is an obvious reason for this: if any genre looks for the universal, the perennial, in human existence, then that genre is satire. The subject of this satire – greed – greed carried to the level of a violent, consuming and bizarre obsession – is of course timeless. One can imagine the agonies our anti-hero, Harper, would have gone through over, for example, 'Midday Money' on the 'Richard and Judy Show', frantically calculating the phone bills on the one hand, weighing up the risks of not trying on the other – and generally twisting himself into avaricious knots. Our era would have suited him, I think. We may not, most of us, be misers, but our fascination (obsession?) with money is undeniable, and amply catered for by our media – vis: 'Who Wants To Be A Millionaire', 'The Weakest Link' (where people are actually prepared to have their self-esteem demolished, perhaps irreparably, for the sake of a couple of grand in the hand) 'Richard and Judy', that advert you may or may not have seen for something called 'equity release', etc etc. To say nothing of the endless leaflets from banks and building societies, now pleading with us to borrow, now badgering us to save, at ever more attractive rates – a plethora of information that causes the modern Harper almost to implode with worry, to turn, scorpion-like, on himself. It sounds pat, but there is a bit of Molière's Harpagon in all of us, today as much as ever, and that is why he has become Harper. So we make no apologies to the purists for choosing a present day setting (and indeed, following the same logic spacially, an English one) and if that has necessitated one or two outrageous tweaks to the text (and I stress, only one or two) well, some might say, so much the better.

On the other hand, we have, I hope, also done justice to the theatrical roots, albeit loosely laid down, of Molière's play – I mean in the *commedia dell'arte*, and perhaps also Roman comedy. There are, in this play, and despite the fact that Molière is aiming at a more sophisticated, psychologically-aware brand of comedy, distinct vestiges of that other comic world, one peopled by stock characters – wily servants, foolish old men, feckless sons and adorable females (too adorable, perhaps, for a modern taste). But, finally, the commedia would never have come up with a brilliant touch like Harpagon's mention, in one of his soliloquys, of how envious he is of people who are able simply to leave their money in bank deposits, where they can earn a nice rate of interest on it! It is a lovely insight into the nature of obesessionality – a man who can clearly see a wiser course, yet is wholly unable to act on his perception, so completely gripped is he by his monomania. Here we are in a different world altogether – that of a very shrewdly-drawn comedy of character more reminiscent of Ben Jonson than Plautus, or Italian farce.

The other play in this volume, *The Idiot* (1655) is Molière's first full-scale comedy, and had its first production in Lyon in 1655, when the playwright was already thirty-three. It is as far removed in character from *The Miser*, almost as it could possibly be. It stands right at the opposite end of the Molière spectrum. Where *The Miser* has a fairly serious satirical and moralising agenda, for all its ostensible insouciance and farcicality, what we have in *The Idiot* is a completely straightforward farce, a French take on Roman comedy and the commedia dell'arte, with stock characters like the wily servant; his amorous, irresponsible, more or less doltish young master; a gullible old man; a rapacious merchant – and so on. As one would expect, being from that stable, it comprises a series of comic set-pieces whose purpose is solely, wholly to amuse. That is not, however, to detract from the play, which is a tour de force in its skilful handling of what is, in essence, a single running gag. And the whole is suffused with an immense winsomeness, a gentle, Terentian humour that is thoroughly engaging. Rarely, one imagines, has disbelief been so cheerfully, charmingly suspended!

Ranjit Bolt
London, 2001

THE MISER

Characters

HARPER
a miser

ELEANOR
his daughter, in love with Victor

VICTOR
his butler, in love with Eleanor

CHARLIE
his son, in love with Marianne

MARIANNE
a poor girl, in love with Charlie

FAY
a matchmaker

MR SIMON
a financial intermediary

FLETCHER
an operator

JACK
Harper's chauffeur-cum-cook

SIR ARTHUR EDGERTON
a tycoon

A DETECTIVE

CLAUDIA/MERVIN
servants in Harper's house

This translation of *The Miser* was first performed at The Chichester Festival Theatre on 26 July 1995, produced by Duncan C Weldon. It was then performed in this version at The Salisbury Playhouse on 20 April 2001, with the following cast:

HARPER, Brian Poyser

CHARLIE, Jamie Bradley

ELEANOR, Fenella Woolgar

VICTOR, Stephen Billington

MARIANNE, Lisa Ellis

FAY, Maggie Norris

FLETCHER/CLAUDE/DETECTIVE, Michael Hodgson

SIR ARTHUR/MERVIN/MR SIMON, Graham Howes

JACK, Shaun Prendergast

Director, Richard Beecham

Designer, Richard Foxton

Lighting Designer, Peter Hunter

Sound Designer, Paul Stear

Assistant Director, Douglas Rintoul

Stage Manager, Julia Reid

ACT ONE

VICTOR: Why so sad, Eleanor? You've made me so happy.
You can't be having second thoughts?

ELEANOR: No, Victor. I'm only afraid I may love you too
much. Not that I can do anything about it.

VICTOR: How can you possibly love me too much? We're
going to married... aren't we?

ELEANOR: Of course. But there's still a serious obstacle.

VICTOR: There is?

ELEANOR: My father. I'm terrified of him.

VICTOR: With good reason.

ELEANOR: What will he think about me marrying his
butler?

VICTOR: Ellie, what does it matter what he thinks, as long
as you love me?

ELEANOR: But what about you? Do you really love me?

VICTOR: How can you ask that?

ELEANOR: You might change your mind. It happens every
day: a girl gives herself to a man, and how does he repay
her? By cooling off.

VICTOR: I'm not like the rest. I'll love you till the day I die.

ELEANOR: Ah, Victor, that's what men always say. It's   .
what they *do* that counts.

VICTOR: But there's no sense in anticipating what's never
going to happen! You'll only cause yourself unnecessary
pain.

ELEANOR: I'm sure you'd never deceive me. I think you
really do love me. I'm still worried about my father,
though. He doesn't see you through my eyes. How could
I help loving you? For one thing, you're the sexiest man
I've ever met. For another, you saved my life.

VICTOR: I wish you'd get rid of this idea that I saved your
life! I got you out of a snowdrift. What was I *supposed* to
do? Leave you there? I only have one claim on your
love, Ellie: I love you.

13

ELEANOR: You risked your *life* for me. And it didn't stop there. After you'd rescued me, you were so sweet, so attentive. I could see that you loved me, truly, deeply. You gave up everything for me. You're happy to work for a tyrannical old skinflint! How could all this fail to make me yours? Naturally I've agreed to be your wife. But the *tyrannical skinflint* may take a different view. And if I marry someone he doesn't like...

VICTOR: (*Wearily.*) I know, I know, the money your uncle settled on you.

ELEANOR: The *million pounds* he settled on me. My father's the sole trustee. And if I marry someone he doesn't approve of, I won't see a penny of it. Till Father dies we'll be poor, when we could have been rolling in it. That doesn't make much sense, does it?

VICTOR: I suppose not. Look: all I want is you. Rich or poor – it's all the same to me...

ELEANOR: You're right, of course. I suppose I shouldn't think about money. It's not essential for happiness. It's not even a guarantee of it.

VICTOR: Too right.

ELEANOR: All the same, it's *easier* to be happy with a million pounds in the bank.

VICTOR: Look, I'm hoping to find my parents soon. If I do, I'm sure your father'll give us his blessing. I should get word of them very soon. If I don't, I intend to go and look for them.

ELEANOR: Don't leave – please. Just concentrate on getting in with my father.

VICTOR: I'm *trying* to get in with him. You saw how I kowtowed to him to get the job. How I pretend to share all his opinions. I'm playing a part the whole time. What's more, it's working like a charm. I've learned how to make a man like you: a) dress to please him; b) praise his faults; c) agree with everything he says; and d) applaud everything he does. You can never overdo flattery. It can be as blatant as you like, and even the cleverest people are highly susceptible to it. You can make someone swallow anything, as long as you help it

down with a little sweet talk. All right, so sincerity's
gone by the board, but he who pays the piper calls the
tune. If crawling's the only way to win him round, whose
fault's that?

ELEANOR: You ought to get my brother on our side.

VICTOR: Charlie? I couldn't handle him and your father at
once. They're such completely different characters. I'd
get my stories mixed up. Why don't *you* work on him?
He ought to take our part. Brotherly love and all that.
He's coming! I'd better go. Talk to him – and don't tell
him any more than you need to.

ELEANOR: I'm not sure I've got the nerve to tell him
anything.

(*Exit VICTOR.*)

CHARLIE: I'm glad I've caught up with you. I *must* speak
to you. I've a secret to tell you.

ELEANOR: I'm all ears.

CHARLIE: It boils down to this: I'm in love. I want to
marry her. But there's a problem.

ELEANOR: Oh, really?! Let me guess...

CHARLIE: The money uncle Charles settled on us. If
Father doesn't approve of my choice...

ELEANOR: Don't go on. I know the rest.

CHARLIE: Then you see my problem.

ELEANOR: I certainly do. (*Beat.*) Are you engaged?

CHARLIE: No. But I intend to be, and you needn't try
dissuading me.

ELEANOR: Why on earth would I want to do that?

CHARLIE: I don't know. You're not in love. You don't
know how violently it affects people. You're always so
damned sensible.

ELEANOR: Sensible! I wish you hadn't said that! We all go
off the rails once in our lives. Wait till I've told you *my*
secret. You'll see I'm no more sensible than you.

CHARLIE: I don't believe it! You mean...?

ELEANOR: You first. Who is she?

CHARLIE: She's just come to live round here. Oh, Ellie,
she's absolutely wonderful. To see her is to love her. Her
name's Marianne. She lives with her mother – a sweet

woman who's always ill. Pretty seriously ill, in fact. She
wants to help her in any way she can – a live-in nurse;
proper hospital care. All that'll come to a small fortune.
Which makes getting uncle Charles's settlement doubly
important. Marianne's so devoted to her. If only you
could see her – waiting on her hand and foot; cheering
her up all the time – you'd be as moved as I am. The
girl's an angel. Everything she does is a delight. She's so
kind; so graceful; so vivacious; so free of all duplicity;
so utterly adorable! I wish you could see her!

ELEANOR: I almost can – you describe her so well. In any
case, you love her. That's all I need to know about her.

CHARLIE: Her mother's delightful too. The point is,
they're none too well off. They're very careful with
money, and even so they barely manage to make ends
meet. They couldn't possibly afford round the clock
nurses, which is really what Marianne's mother needs.
Oh, Ellie, imagine the happiness! To rescue the girl you
love from penury. To help a good, kind woman in her
hour of need. And then picture my anger at being *denied*
that happiness – robbed of the chance to show Marianne
how much she means to me – by Father's miserliness.

ELEANOR: I can picture it all too vividly.

CHARLIE: No you can't! I'm beside myself! What could be
crueller than his meanness towards us? If *we* were plants
and *money* was water, we'd be dead by now. What's the
use of having settlements, and a rich father, if we're
penniless while we're young? That's why I had to speak
to you. I'm going to sound Father out – about Marianne,
I mean. And I want you to help me. If he doesn't
approve, I've decided to go away with her. We'll have to
take our chances abroad somewhere. I'll need money for
that. I'm looking all over the place for a loan. If you're
in love too, and if he's against both our choices, we'll just
have to leave him. It's high time we escaped his tyranny.
The man's not a miser – he's a monster!

ELEANOR: It's true. Every day he gives us more reason to
mourn Mother's death. I don't...

CHARLIE: He's coming! Let's go. There's a lot to do.
We've simply *got* to break him down.

(*They go. Enter HARPER and FLETCHER.*)

HARPER: Be off with you! At once! Don't say a word, just go, NOW, you scrofulous scumbag!

FLETCHER: (*Aside.*) What a horrible old man! I've never met anyone like him! If you ask me, he's completely mad.

HARPER: What's that, you etiolated little twerp? What are you muttering about?

FLETCHER: Why are you getting rid of me?

HARPER: Questions, questions! You never stop. Scram, or I'll kill you!

FLETCHER: But what have I done?!

HARPER: Just GET OUT OF HERE!

FLETCHER: Your son wanted to see me about something.

HARPER: Wait for him in the street, then! I won't have you hanging about here, eyes peeled for the main chance. You're always spying on me. I'm sick of it. I don't trust you. You watch me all the time. You're after every sodding thing I own. I can see it in your eyes. You're always on the look out for something to steal.

FLETCHER: How the hell am I supposed to steal from you? You keep everything locked away, and stand guard over it day and night.

HARPER: I'll lock things away if I like – *and* stand guard over them. I'm surrounded by informers. They watch my every move. (*Aside.*) The pilfering pisswit knows about my money! (*Aloud.*) You're going to tell everyone aren't you?

FLETCHER: Tell them what?

HARPER: That I've got money hidden away.

FLETCHER: You *have?!*

HARPER: I didn't say that! (*Aside.*) I could murder him! (*Aloud.*) What I'm asking is: have you been spreading rumours? About my money?

FLETCHER: Why should I care whether you've got money or not?

HARPER: Don't you come the smart-arse with *me* or I'll flay you to within an inch of your worthless, godforsaken life! (*He raises his hand.*) Now, for the last time: OUT!

FLETCHER: All right, all right, I'm on my way!

HARPER: Hang on a goddamn minute! What are you taking with you?

FLETCHER: With me?

HARPER: Come here! Hold out your hands.

(*FLETCHER holds out one hand.*)

HARPER: And the other one.

FLETCHER: Other what?

HARPER: HAND!! What did you think I meant? Foot?

(*FLETCHER holds out the other hand.*)

HARPER: What about your trousers?

FLETCHER: See for yourself.

(*HARPER rummages in FLETCHER's trousers.*)

HARPER: Ideal for thieves, trousers like these. Whoever makes them deserves to be shot. You could have anything stashed in here.

FLETCHER: (*Aside.*) It'd serve him right if he *was* robbed. I've a good mind to do it myself.

HARPER: Eh?

FLETCHER: What?

HARPER: I distinctly heard the word 'robbed'.

FLETCHER: I said you were checking to see if I'd robbed you.

(*HARPER feels in FLETCHER's pockets.*)

FLETCHER: Misers! Scum of the earth!

HARPER: What was that?

FLETCHER: I said: 'Misers! Scum of the earth!'

HARPER: Meaning who?

FLETCHER: Meaning misers. Who did you think I meant?

HARPER: Never mind what I thought. Who are you talking to anyway?

FLETCHER: My hat.

HARPER: I'll give you hat, you rapacious, mendacious, predacious BUM! (*Raising his hand.*)

FLETCHER: Hey! What's wrong with cursing misers?

HARPER: Nothing. But you talk too much and you're insolent. Now shut up.

FLETCHER: I didn't name any names.

HARPER: One more word and I'll give you such a thrashing *you'll* be in a wheelchair for the rest of your days.

FLETCHER: If the cap fits...
HARPER: I SAID...
FLETCHER: All right, all right...
   (*HARPER plunges a hand into one of FLETCHER's trouser pockets.*)
HARPER: (*Thinks he's found something.*) Ah! (*Finds he's wrong.*) Ooh.
   (*FLETCHER turns out the other pocket.*)
FLETCHER: Satisfied?
HARPER: I've had enough of this. Just give it back.
FLETCHER: What?
HARPER: Whatever it was you took.
FLETCHER: I haven't taken anything.
HARPER: Cross your heart?
FLETCHER: And hope to die.
HARPER: Oh, to hell with you.
FLETCHER: I'll be off, then.
HARPER: You must do as your conscience dictates.
   (*FLETCHER goes.*)
   Snivelling cur! Can't stand the sight of him. It's no joke having lots of money in the house. But I don't trust banks. It's a nightmare finding a good hiding place. I don't trust safes either. They're an invitation to burglars. They always make a beeline for them. But I'm not happy with holes in the garden either. I've hidden a hundred grand in one.
   (*Enter ELEANOR and CHARLIE, talking in low voices.*)
HARPER: Oh God! I've gone and given myself away! What is it?
CHARLIE: Nothing, Father.
HARPER: How long have you been lurking there?
CHARLIE: We haven't.
HARPER: You didn't hear...?
CHARLIE: Hear what?
HARPER: Er...
ELEANOR: Yes?
HARPER: What I was saying just then.
CHARLIE: No.
HARPER: Oh yes you did.
ELEANOR: Excuse *me*, but we didn't.

HARPER: You must have heard some of it. I was talking to myself. I was saying how money's incredibly hard to come by these days. Must be amazing, I said, to have – say – a hundred grand around the place.

CHARLIE: We weren't sure if we should interrupt you or not.

HARPER: On the contrary, I'm glad I can put you straight. I wouldn't want you thinking I had a hundred grand here myself.

CHARLIE: We've no wish to nose into your affairs.

HARPER: I would to God I *did* have a hundred grand.

CHARLIE: I don't believe...

HARPER: My troubles would be over.

ELEANOR: There are some things...

HARPER: I could really use a sum like that.

CHARLIE: I think...

HARPER: I'd be in clover.

ELEANOR: You're not exactly...

HARPER: Wouldn't be complaining about hard times *then!*

CHARLIE: For goodness' sake, Father, what have you got to worry about? Everyone knows you're loaded.

HARPER: Loaded? Loaded! Whoever told you that's a liar. It's balls. They should electrocute people who go around spreading rumours like that!

ELEANOR: Don't get in a tizz.

HARPER: I don't know! My own children turning against me! What next?

CHARLIE: Turning against you? We said you had money, that's all.

HARPER: But to say such things – spend money the way you do – it makes people think I'm a bloody millionaire. One day someone'll burgle me and cut my throat. Then you'll be sorry.

CHARLIE: What do you mean, spend money the way I do?

HARPER: You know perfectly well what I'm referring to: conspicuous expenditure. I blew *her* up about it yesterday. But you're even worse. It's a scandal. If you took the money you spend in a year and invested it instead, you could make a tidy bit of interest. I've told you a hundred times, I don't like the way you carry on. The *clothes* you wear, for instance.

CHARLIE: I've bought precisely one item of clothing in the last three years: these trainers.

HARPER: And just look at them. I've never seen anything so flashy.

CHARLIE: Flashy! I got them at the Oxfam shop.

HARPER: I reckon you must be stealing from me.

CHARLIE: Stealing from you?!

HARPER: How else could you support such a life-style?

CHARLIE: What life-style?

HARPER: The fast cars...

CHARLIE: A second hand deux chevaux?

HARPER: The meals out.

CHARLIE: At Burger King?

HARPER: You shouldn't eat out at all. You should put your money on deposit – build up a nice little nest egg.

CHARLIE: Oh, really? What with?

HARPER: Let's change the subject. (*Aside.*) They're making signs to one another! They want to pinch my wallet! (*Aloud.*) What do those gesticulations mean?

ELEANOR: We're deciding who should speak first. We've both got something to tell you.

HARPER: And *I've* got something to tell *you*.

CHARLIE: It's about marriage.

HARPER: Snap!

ELEANOR: OH!!

HARPER: What's that OH!! in aid of? What's frightening about marriage?

CHARLIE: It depends what you have in mind. We're afraid you mightn't agree with our choices.

HARPER: Don't jump the gun. You'll have no cause to complain. Now: have either of you come across a girl called Marianne? She lives nearby.

CHARLIE: Yes.

HARPER: And you?

ELEANOR: I've heard people talk about her.

HARPER: (*To CHARLIE.*) What do you make of her?

CHARLIE: She's an absolute marvel.

HARPER: What about her looks?

CHARLIE: She's beautiful.

HARPER: And her manner?

CHARLIE: Open; spirited – quite delightful.

HARPER: A girl like that deserves a lot of attention, wouldn't you say?

CHARLIE: Absolutely.

HARPER: She's quite a catch for any man.

CHARLIE: She certainly is.

HARPER: Just the kind of girl you'd want to run your household.

CHARLIE: Undoubtedly.

HARPER: She'd give her husband satisfaction, no?

CHARLIE: She would indeed.

HARPER: There's just one little problem: she's not as well off as one would like.

CHARLIE: What difference does *that* make? She's a girl in a million.

HARPER: *Without* a million, don't you mean? Never mind – there's bound to be *some* way of getting money out of her.

CHARLIE: Doubtless.

HARPER: I'm glad you agree. She's a decent, good-natured girl. Her mother seems to like me, too. She's an invalid, and I'm not saying I mightn't even see my way to shelling out the odd quid on medical care and so on. Least I can do. So I reckon it's in the bag. Marianne's devoted to her. She won't pass up a chance like this to help the old cow out. As long as she brings some money with her somehow, I'm going to marry her.

CHARLIE: YOU'RE going to marry her!

HARPER: Yes. Do you have a problem with that?

CHARLIE: B-b-b-but... YOU?!

HARPER: Yes: me! me! me!

CHARLIE: I don't feel at all well suddenly. I'm going.

HARPER: Can't be anything serious. Go and get yourself a glass of water.

(*CHARLIE goes.*)

HARPER: Not just a ponce – a pansy, too! Well, Marianne, that's the wife I've chosen.

ELEANOR: You make it sound as though you've been shopping!

HARPER: While we're on the subject of shopping, isn't it high time someone took *you* off the shelf? Seriously, I'm anxious about you. Your biological clock must be ticking away like nobody's business.

ELEANOR: What *are* you on about? I'm barely twenty!

HARPER: True. All the same, you must have given the matter some thought.

ELEANOR: On the contrary, I haven't given it any thought at all.

HARPER: You surprise me. Anyway, be that as it may, I think I've got a candidate you might find agreeable.

ELEANOR: You have?

HARPER: Yes. My friend Sir Arthur Edgerton.

ELEANOR: Sir Arthur Edgerton?!

HARPER: That's right. He's a solid, sensible man. Can't be more than fifty. More to the point, I'm told he's rolling in it. He bought yet another department store the other day. He'll look after you better than I could... even.

ELEANOR: I know where you're coming from. You don't want to keep me any more. Getting rid of me'll be another of your economies. I'm right aren't I?

HARPER: That's an unbelievably hurtful thing to say, after all I've done for you!

ELEANOR: It's true, though. Well I'm not planning on marrying, Father, if it's all the same to you. And if I do decide to get hitched, it won't be to a fat, fifty-year-old business man.

HARPER: What if I want you to?

ELEANOR: Too bad.

HARPER: That's what *you* think.

ELEANOR: I'm sorry, but I'm *not* having Sir Arthur.

HARPER: Yes you are.

ELEANOR: No I'm not. I think you must be living on some other planet. Since when is it any of your business who I marry.

HARPER: Oh, I think it is...

(*He is evidently thinking of the marriage settlement. ELEANOR falls silent for a moment.*)

ELEANOR: (*Uncertain.*) You must be mad... if you think you can just... lumber me with a husband against my will...

HARPER: Mad, eh? We'll see about that.

ELEANOR: 'Lady Edgerton'! Yuck! I'd rather die.

HARPER: You'll live, and you'll marry him. But how dare you be so bolshy with *me?* I'm your father, for Christ's sake.

ELEANOR: You can't *force* me to marry anyone. You've no legal right.

HARPER: I think Edgerton's an excellent choice. What's more, I'm sure everyone will agree.

ELEANOR: I should think anyone remotely reasonable will *dis*agree.

HARPER: Here comes Victor. Shall we let *him* decide?

ELEANOR: All right.

HARPER: You'll abide by what he says?

ELEANOR: I will.

HARPER: Splendid! Then it's settled.

(*Enter VICTOR.*)

HARPER: Come here, Victor. We want you to decide something.

VICTOR: You must be right, sir.

HARPER: Do you know what we're discussing?

VICTOR: No. But you can't possibly be wrong. You're never wrong about anything.

HARPER: I want her to marry someone. He's rich; he's wise. And the little bitch tells me – to my face – that she won't have him. What do you make of that?

VICTOR: What do I make of it?

HARPER: Yes.

VICTOR: Well... I... er...

HARPER: Hmmmm...?

VICTOR: Well – I agree with you in principle. Like I say, you're never wrong about anything. On the other hand, she might just possibly have a point. You see...

HARPER: What's this? Sir Arthur's an extremely eligible man. He's kind, sensible, very well connected and possibly one of the ten richest men in the country. What's more, he's got no children by his first wife. How could I... she do better?

VICTOR: All that's true. But mightn't she just *possibly* be justified in saying you're rushing things a bit? That you should at least give her time? To come round to your way of thinking? Indeed, she *might* even argue...

HARPER: Argue what?

VICTOR: That *in this day and age,* and all that, it's not really your decision.

HARPER: Stuff 'this day and age'! We have to seize on this opportunity. The man's another Branson in the making. Who knows how much we might screw out of him?

VICTOR: Another Branson, eh?

HARPER: Yes.

VICTOR: I see. Well, there's no arguing with money. Of course, Ellie... your daughter... *could* perhaps point out that marriage is an extremely serious matter; that it's a question of being happy or miserable for the rest of your life; that you should think long and hard before entering into a liaison that lasts till the grave...

HARPER: Look, Victor, we're talking *mega-rich* here.

VICTOR: You're right. There's nothing more to be said...
I suppose some people might say that the age gap in this case – not to mention the difference in tastes and temperament – could lead to some nasty trouble.

HARPER: Mega *mega* rich...

VICTOR: Subject closed... On the other *haaand* – assuming for a moment that this *is* your decision – I imagine there might be fathers – I mean it's entirely plausible – who'd put a daughter's happiness before the chance of making a quid or two. Who'd think the crucial factor in a marriage is compatibility – that's if it's going to last – and be harmonious – and happy – with no infidelities on either side – and...

HARPER: Mega mega m...

VICTOR: Yes, that settles it.

HARPER: (*Looking out towards the garden.*) Hey! Did I hear a dog bark? Someone's after my money! Wait there! (*Goes.*)

ELEANOR: What were you playing at, agreeing with him like that?

VICTOR: If we upset him we won't get what we want. Some people simply can't be reasoned with. You have to play them like fish – agree with everything they say, and *then...*

ELEANOR: But Sir Arthur Edgerton!

VICTOR: He can't force you.

ELEANOR: That's what I told him.

VICTOR: We'll just have to make him drop the idea somehow.

HARPER: (*Re-entering.*) It was nothing.

VICTOR: If all else fails, we can... (*Sees HARPER.*) Absobloodylutely! Your father's an extremely wise man and you must respect his wishes. Sir Arthur's rich. *Mega* rich.

HARPER: Well said!

VICTOR: I'm sorry, sir. I got a bit carried away. I was giving her a piece of my mind.

HARPER: Don't apologise! That's precisely what I want. In fact, as of now I'm officially appointing you her minder. I want you to keep her in check. (*To ELEANOR.*) Where are you off to? Victor's a second father to you now. You're to do everything he says.

VICTOR: (*To ELEANOR.*) Ah, yes! You'd better not cross swords with *me!*

(*ELEANOR moves away.*)

VICTOR: I'll stay with her, sir. I haven't finished my little lecture yet.

HARPER: Good *man!* The fact is...

VICTOR: I'll keep her in check, all right!

HARPER: Do that. We must definitely...

VICTOR: Relax, sir. You can count on me.

HARPER: I trust you implicitly. Now, I'm going out for some air. I'll be back soon.

VICTOR: (*To ELEANOR.*) Yes, cash is what counts. You should thank Heaven for sending you a father like yours. He knows what life's about, he does. A rich husband? Look no further. Money beats looks, youth, class, wisdom and character put together.

HARPER: What an excellent fellow! Spoken like a guru! Such wisdom – from a menial. He'll make her come round. My problems are at an end. (*Goes.*)

End of Act One.

ACT TWO

CHARLIE, FLETCHER.

CHARLIE: Where the hell have you been? Didn't I tell you to...

FLETCHER: I was waiting for you here when your father chased me away. What a tetchy old turd he is! I almost got a beating.

CHARLIE: Any news about the loan? I'm more desperate than ever. Guess what happened the other day?

FLETCHER: Tell me.

CHARLIE: He caught me in Tesco, buying a meat samosa, and he made me put it back. Threatened to disinherit me if I didn't.

FLETCHER: Hmmm. Seems a bit harsh.

CHARLIE: But I'm used to that kind of madness from him. It's nothing compared to what I've just found out.

FLETCHER: Let's hear the worst.

HARPER: He's after Marianne. He wants to marry her.

FLETCHER: Who? Your father?! He must be insane.

CHARLIE: Disgusting, isn't it?

FLETCHER: What does he think he's playing at? Who's he trying to fool? Monsters like him weren't made to chase young girls.

CHARLIE: He's besotted with her. It's just my luck.

FLETCHER: Why not tell him about...?

CHARLIE: I daren't. Not yet. There must be easier ways to stop this marriage. If I could only get that wretched loan. Have you made any progress?

FLETCHER: Funny you should say that. I bumped into a bloke in the pub the other day by the name of Simon. He said an acquaintance of his had some spare cash on his hands and was looking to lend it out. It seems he's local. I've arranged a meeting.

CHARLIE: I'll get the ten grand I'm after?

FLETCHER: Yes. But there are some strings attached.

CHARLIE: You didn't mention my name?

FLETCHER: Of course not.

CHARLIE: Have you spoken to the lender?

FLETCHER: It seems he's as secretive as you. I've no idea who he is. He wants to meet you in a hotel room. You're to tell him your financial position, and who your family are. The mention of your father should remove any obstacles. Now, about those strings, I've got a whole list of them here. (*He produces a document and reads.*) 'Assuming that the lender sees all the securities, and that the borrower is of age, and from a family with substantial means, comprising reliable assets, wholly unencumbered, a detailed agreement will be drawn up in the presence of a solicitor of impeccable credentials. Said solicitor, for the purposes of said agreement, to be selected by the lender, he being at greater risk in this transaction.'

CHARLIE: There's not a lot I can say to that.

FLETCHER: 'In order to retain a clear conscience, the lender intends to ask for interest of five per cent.'

CHARLIE: The man's a saint!

FLETCHER: 'However, since said lender does not have the requisite sum in ready moneys and, in order to satisfy the borrower, is obliged to borrow himself at the rate of twenty per cent, it is agreed that the first said borrower will pay that interest, in addition to the aforementioned five per cent, without prejudice to any other of the above conditions, it being understood that it is only in order to satisfy the first said borrower that the lender, or second said borrower, is obliged to borrow secondarily in the first place.'

CHARLIE: The man's a swine!

FLETCHER: Yes.

CHARLIE: But I need the money so I'll have to accept the terms.

FLETCHER: That's what I told Mr Simon.

CHARLIE: Any more 'strings'?

FLETCHER: One or two. 'The lender can raise only five thousand of the ten thousand pounds required in ready moneys. As regards the remaining five thousand, it is agreed that the borrower will accept the various goods

and chattels itemised below, on which the lender has
placed the fairest possible valuations.'

CHARLIE: What the hell's all that about?!

FLETCHER: Wait till you've heard the items. 'Item: one
video recorder (reconditioned). Item: two stuffed
antelope. Item: six wicker garden chairs (nearly new).
Item: one chamber pot (antique).'

CHARLIE: What am I meant to do with junk like that?

FLETCHER: 'Items: one angler's bivouac (plastic) and one
angler's pole (fibre glass; nearly new). Item: one copy of
Alan Clarke's memoirs. Item: one Rick Astley CD. Item:
Two and a half tons of coarse-grained gravel. Item:....'

CHARLIE: All right, all right, I think I've got the point.
He's a shit. A twenty carat shit. Not content with
charging an exorbitant rate of interest, he fobs me off
with the contents of his attic and values it at five
thousand pounds! But what can I do. He's got me by the
short and curlies, the sod!

FLETCHER: You're on the primrose path, sir, if you don't
mind my saying so – living on credit, buying dear,
selling cheap, and generally eating your corn in the
blade.

CHARLIE: What do you want me to do? This is what
young men are reduced to by miserly fathers. And then
people are shocked when their sons wish them dead.

FLETCHER: Yours would try the patience of a saint, I grant
you. I'm not the criminal type – well, not really – but
I'm here to tell you that the way that bastard carries on
makes me think of robbing him, and I reckon I'd be
doing a good deed, at that.

CHARLIE: Let's have another look at that inventory.
(*Enter HARPER and SIMON.*)

SIMON: He's desperate for money, all right. He'll accept
any terms.

HARPER: You're sure there's no risk? Who are his family?
Have they got money?

SIMON: I've no detailed information. In fact I found the
fellow quite by chance. He'll fill you in himself. The
middleman assured me you wouldn't be disappointed.

I've reason to believe that his family's extremely rich,
and he's ready to guarantee that his father will die in
within the year.
HARPER: (*Rubbing his hands together.*) Excellent! Well, we
must help people when we can. It's only Christian charity.
SIMON: Of course.
FLETCHER: My god! There he is!
CHARLIE: Who?
FLETCHER: Our Mr Simon. What the hell's he doing
here?
CHARLIE: He's found out who I am and where I live!
(*Menacing.*) Look here, Fletcher, if you've blown our
cover...
SIMON: (*Seeing CHARLIE and FLETCHER, and to
CHARLIE.*) My God! You're in a hurry, sir! Who told
you he lived here? (*To HARPER.*) It wasn't me, Mr
Harper, I promise you. Anyway, I don't suppose it much
matters. These gentlemen are very discreet. You may as
well sort everything out now.
HARPER: Eh? Sort what out?
SIMON: This is the gentleman who wants to borrow the ten
thousand.
HARPER: (*To CHARLIE.*) What's this, you swine?! So
you're the one resorting to these reckless tactics!
CHARLIE: So it's you that's screwing people like this!
HARPER: So it's you that wants to ruin himself by taking
out reckless loans.
CHARLIE: So it's you that wants to enrich himself with
criminal usury.
HARPER: How dare you face me after this?
CHARLIE: How dare you face *anyone* after this?
HARPER: Have you no shame? The profligacy! You must
be spending like a madman! It's a disgrace! You're
frittering away all my hard-earned cash.
CHARLIE: Have *I* no shame?! You're forfeiting all claim to
respectability, lending on terms like these. Piling up
money – that's all that matters to you. You're worse than
the worst loan shark.
HARPER: Out of my sight, you little shit!

CHARLIE: Which is the greater crime? Borrowing money
you need, or stealing – yes, *stealing* money you're not
going to use?

HARPER: I said, out! I can't bear to listen to you.

(*CHARLIE and MR SIMON go.*)

HARPER: I'm not all that upset about this. It's a timely
wake up call. I'm going to keep a closer eye on him
than ever.

(*Enter FAY.*)

FAY: Ah! Mr Harper...

HARPER: Time to check my cash. Be with you in a
minute, Fay. (*Goes.*)

FLETCHER: (*To audience.*) What a hilarious episode! He
must have no end of junk stashed away. I didn't
recognise a single item on that list.

FAY: Morning, Fletcher. You look very shifty. What you
up to?

FLETCHER: I could ask you the same question.

FAY: Oh, the usual thing: wheeler-dealing; fixing things for
people; making the most of my meagre talents. You've
got to be smart just to get by these days. Intrigue and
hard work – how else can I make a living?

FLETCHER: You've got some business with the master of
the house?

FAY: Yes. I'm handling a little business deal for him. There
should be a little something in it for me.

FLETCHER: You won't get a red cent out of *him*. Unless
you're a smarter woman than I took you for. Money's
hard to come by in this house.

FAY: Maybe. But there are deals and deals.

FLETCHER: I'm sorry, but you don't know Harper. He's
the least human human being in the whole of humanity.
There's no one as hardhearted or as tightfisted. No
matter what you do for him, he won't cough up. Insults?
He'll give you more than you'll know what to do with.
But money? Forget it. Why, he's so mean he doesn't even
give his word – he lends it.

FAY: Ah, but I know how to handle people. I can find their
weak spots and tickle them.

31

FLETCHER: Bollocks! I defy you to get a penny out of
him. You could be starving to death and he wouldn't lift
a finger. He doesn't care what people think of him. He's
not interested in being kind, or good. He's obsessed with
money. Ask him for fifty p and he goes into convulsions.
You might just as well stick a knife in him and rip his
guts out. If you... He's coming back. I'm off. (*Goes.*)
(*Enter HARPER.*)

HARPER: Excellent! Every last penny present and correct.
Now, Fay, what can I do you for?

FAY: (*Instant sycophancy.*) Oh, Mr Harper, you're looking so
well! You're the absolute picture of health.

HARPER: You must be joking.

FAY: I'm serious – you look better now than I've ever seen
you. I've met blokes half your age that looked older.

HARPER: Fay, I'm seventy, for Heaven's sake.

FAY: So? What's seventy these days? You're about to enter
your prime!

HARPER: True. All the same, it'd be nice to enter it twenty
years younger.

FAY: I'll lay even money you'll live to be a hundred.

HARPER: You think so?

FAY: I know so. It's written all over you. Let's have a look
at you. Give us a quick twirl. (*Peering up close.*) *And*
you've got the mark of long life. Just here – under your
left nostril.

HARPER: You can spot that, can you?

FAY: *Oh,* yes. Show me your right hand. Christ, what a life
line!

HARPER: Eh?

FAY: That line there. See how long it is?

HARPER: So? What does that signify?

FAY: Did I say a hundred? Add twenty.

HARPER: That's impossible.

FAY: I tell you, they're going to have to kill you if they
want you to die. You'll bury your children *and* your
grandchildren.

HARPER: I can't wait. Now: what about our little
transaction? How's it going?

FAY: Need you ask? When did I ever not give satisfaction?
Marriages are my forte. You want two people spliced? I'll
splice them. I could get Liam and Patsy back together.
But this one's a doddle. I see a lot of these two. I bend
their ears about you all the time.

HARPER: What does the mother say?

FAY: She's over the moon about the idea.

HARPER: So you reckon it's in the bag?

FAY: Definitely. Marianne'd marry a baboon if it'd help her
beloved mother.

HARPER: A baboon? Are you implying...?

FAY: Oh, no comparison intended, I assure you.

HARPER: Just you watch your step. Look here: I was
rather hoping Marianne might come and dine with us
tonight. I'm having Sir Arthur over.

FAY: Good idea. And before dinner perhaps she could call
on your daughter. Go on a shopping spree with her.

HARPER: A window shopping spree. Excellent idea! They
can take the car.

FAY: That'd be nice.

HARPER: But, Fay, have you discussed money with the
mother? She must make an effort. Marianne can't
possibly come with nothing.

FAY: Nothing?! She'll bring you the best part of twenty
thousand pounds a year.

HARPER: Could be worse.

FAY: To begin with, she eats like a bird. She's used to
making do with a little salad; a bit of cheese; a glass of
milk; an apple or two... So you won't have to spend
much on food. None of your expensive delis and wine
shops and what have you. Give her a cut price
supermarket and she's happy. That's worth – what? – five
thousand a year? Then there's her taste in clothes. It's
extremely simple. You won't be splashing out on
designer dresses. TK. Maxx'll do for *her*. She doesn't go
in for jewellery either, unless it's out of a Christmas
cracker. And she won't get people in to rag-roll your
walls, or start bullying you to buy expensive furniture.
I reckon all that comes to at least another five grand.

HARPER: That's all very well, but it's purely hypothetical.

FAY: Excuse *me*, but I don't call not wanting expensive clothes hypothetical. Or not wanting jewellery. A simple, economical marriage is worth its weight in gold. You're hard to please, I must say! What do you want her to do? Take in laundry?

HARPER: That's not a bad idea! Anyway, if you ask me, what she's not going to spend doesn't count as money. It's like giving a receipt for something you haven't sold. I need something concrete.

FAY: You'll get it. She has land abroad somewhere.

HARPER: I'd better look into that. But something else is troubling me. The girl's young, and young people normally go for someone their own age. I'm afraid I may be too old for her. That could lead to – how shall I put this? – goings on – nasty goings on.

FAY: You don't know her. There's something I haven't told you: she hates boys her own age – can't stand the sight of them. She's obsessed with older men.

HARPER: She is?

FAY: Yes. You should hear her on the subject. Know what drives her wild? A man of seventy or more, with a white beard and specs and false teeth. The older the better, as far as she's concerned. Don't try to make yourself look younger than you are. As a matter of fact, seventy's her lower limit. Only about a month ago she broke off an engagement when she found out her fiancé'd been lying about his age. He was only fifty-six.

HARPER: That was the only reason?

FAY: The main one. The other problem was, he didn't wear spectacles.

HARPER: Well, all this is news to *me*.

FAY: There's more. You should see the pin-ups in her room. Leonardo Di Caprio? Robbie Williams? West Life? Not a bit of it. It's Nelson Mandela; the Pope; and the two Alberts.

HARPER: The two Alberts?

FAY: Schweitzer and Einstein.

HARPER: That's wonderful! Who'd have thought it? Come
to think of it, if I were a woman I wouldn't go for young
men either.

FAY: I should think not.

HARPER: I don't know what girls see in them.

FAY: They must be mad. I tell you: young blokes today are
all sissies.

HARPER: That's what I'm always saying. They make me
sick, with their pony tales and their poncy clothes and
their mobile phones. It's obscene.

FAY: They're not a patch on you. What a man! It does my
heart good just to look at you! That build! The way
you're dressed! Who wouldn't fall for you?

HARPER: You think I'm attractive?

FAY: Oh, *what?!* You're a dish. You should be a male model.
Turn this way a bit. Excellent! Now, give us a quick
twirl. What elegance, what grace! And so casual! So
relaxed! You're a fine figure of a man, Mr Harper.

HARPER: Well I'm not decrepit, certainly. My legs aren't
quite what they used to be, but...

FAY: That's nothing. In fact, it'll be a plus with Marianne.

HARPER: Has she seen me yet? You know – in the
neighbourhood?

FAY: No. But we've talked about you a lot. I showed her that
photo of you. And I've given you a hell of a plug – told
her what a wonderful catch you are.

HARPER: You've done well. I'm very grateful to you.

FAY: Can I ask a little favour?

(*HARPER looks severe.*)

I'm about to lose my lawsuit. I just need a bit of money
and everything'll be okay.

(*Silence from HARPER – he frowns.*)

You won't believe how happy Marianne'll be to see you.

(*HARPER brightens again.*)

She'll love those tatty tweeds you wear. Not to mention
your holey old cardy. And as for the watch and chain!
She'll go crazy for you.

HARPER: You certainly know what to say!

FAY: Sir, this lawsuit's really important.

(*HARPER looks angry.*)
If I lose it I'm ruined... She went into ecstasies when I told her about you.
(*HARPER brightens up again.*)
I wish you could've seen her.

HARPER: Fay, I'm overjoyed. I'm in your debt, I really am.

FAY: Please, Gerald – may I call you Gerald?
(*HARPER looks angry again.*)
Please, Gerald, just a teensy bit of... assistance... to put me back on my feet.

HARPER: I'd better be off. I have some letters to write.

FAY: You'd be getting me out of the worst hole I've ever been in.

HARPER: I'll have my car ready to take you and the girls to the shops.

FAY: I'm in desperate straits, or I wouldn't be asking.

HARPER: I must go.
(*Phone rings, off.*)
And there's the phone, too. (*Calling back to her as he goes.*)
Tara!

FAY: I hope you catch a nasty disease from it, you parsimonious old git! Talk about tightfisted! I've seen clams that were more open. He just wouldn't crack. Still, I'm not giving up on this one just yet. I'm bound to get something out of the mother.

End of Act Two.

ACT THREE

HARPER: Come here, all of you. Let me give you your
    instructions. Claudia, I'll start with you.
    (*CLAUDIA comes forward and makes a little bow.*)
    I see you've brought the hoover with you. Excellent.
    (I suggest a pretty prehistoric hoover.) I want you to
    vacuum the whole house. And be careful not to bash the
    furniture. Then you can look after the bottle during
    dinner.
CLAUDIA: Bottle?
HARPER: Bottles, then. But no more than two. And if either
    of them walks, or gets broken, I'll dock your wages.
JACK: (*Aside.*) Wages! He gets these two from a youth
    opportunities scheme.
HARPER: Now, Mervin, you're to wash the glasses and
    pour the wine. Don't pour anyone anything unless
    they're thirsty. And don't do what they do in restaurants.
MERVIN: What's that, sir?
HARPER: Encourage people to have more when they don't
    really want it. Wait till you're asked... twice... and have
    a jug of water ready for diluting.
JACK: (*Aside.*) Wouldn't want anyone enjoying themselves,
    now, would we?
MERVIN: Can we put clean jackets on, sir?
HARPER: Yes – but not till the guests arrive. I don't want
    any more dry-cleaning bills.
CLAUDIA: My skirt's got a huge wine stain on it, sir.
MERVIN: And my trousers are split at the back. People'll
    see my...
HARPER: Just stand with your back to the wall. (*To
    CLAUDIA.*) As for you, you can wear an apron over the
    wine stain. Eleanor, you're in charge of the leavings. And
    don't go putting them down the waste disposal. Claude
    can survive for a week on them. (*To ELEANOR.*) And

you, get ready to welcome Marianne. You're going window shopping with her this afternoon.

ELEANOR: (*Ironic.*) Window-shopping? Oh, goodee! Whereabouts?

HARPER: Nowhere too far. Petrol costs a fortune these days. There are plenty of smart shops in the neighbourhood.

HARPER: (*To CHARLIE.*) Well now, young man, I've forgiven you this morning's episode, but just you mind you put a good face on things for Marianne.

CHARLIE: How d'you mean?

HARPER: Oh, come on! As if one doesn't know how children behave with their stepmothers. You want me to forget your latest prank? Then you'll be politeness personified.

CHARLIE: I can't pretend I'm delighted that she's going to be my stepmother. As for 'putting a good face on things', I'll be doing it all evening, I assure you.

HARPER: Tread carefully, that's all. Victor, keep an eye on him. Now – last but not least – Jack.

JACK: Which am I, sir – chauffeur or cook?

HARPER: Both.

JACK: Which first?

HARPER: Cook.

JACK: Hang on a sec. (*He whips off his chauffeur's cap and dons his chef's hat.*)

HARPER: What the hell do you think...?

JACK: Fire away, sir.

HARPER: I want this dinner party to go with a swing. You'll do us proud, eh?

JACK: If you give me the money.

HARPER: Money! Money! Always bloody money! It's an obsession round here!

VICTOR: I've never heard such impertinence, sir. Any one can give a good dinner party if they splash out. It's a doddle. Now, doing it for next to nothing – that takes real skill.

JACK: A good dinner party for next to nothing!

VICTOR: Yup.

JACK: You must show us your secret. Why not do the
cooking while you're at it. You seem to think
everything's your business round here.

HARPER: Shut up! What will we need?

JACK: Ask him. He'll do you a cut-price job.

HARPER: I'm asking *you*.

JACK: All right: how many will you be?

HARPER: Eight or ten. Say eight. What does for eight will
do for ten, as my mother used to say.

VICTOR: How true.

JACK: Well, you'll want canapés before they sit down –
smoked salmon, caviar, that sort of thing.

HARPER: Caviar? Are you sure?

JACK: Then at least four soups; plenty of hors d'oeuvre;
five main entrees; several puddings; cheeses; cognac;
armagnac; calvados; cointreau; benedictine...

HARPER: What the Devil...?!

JACK: There'll have to be a roast, of course. I could do you
a whole roast boar...

HARPER: I said eight or ten people – not the whole
sodding borough!

JACK: Now, ideally...

HARPER: (*Putting a hand over JACK's mouth.*) You'll ruin me!

JACK: Ideally, we'll want quite a few side dishes.

HARPER: Side dishes on top!

JACK: No, at the side.

VICTOR: Do you want them all to die from overeating?
Where have you been for the past decade? Ask any
doctor about diet.

HARPER: He's right.

VICTOR: You might as well be throwing a suicide party.
We must show some consideration for the guests. *Cuisine
minceur* – that's what we want. Was it David Frost or Dr
Johnson who said: 'Eat to live – don't live to eat.'

HARPER: What wise words! Come here – I want to hug
you! I've never heard anything so apposite – 'Eat to live
– don't live to eat.' Good old David Frost. Write it down
for me, would you? I'm going to have it blazoned in
giant letters in the dining room.

VICTOR: Will do. As for dinner, let me take care of it. I'll do the necessary.

HARPER: Go ahead.

JACK: Fine. Less work for me.

HARPER: We need things to take away people's appetite. Filling things. Cabbage and potato soup, for instance; and lots of stodgy meatloaf; not forgetting *crapeau dans le trou*.

JACK: I *beg* your pardon?

HARPER: Toad in the hole to you.

VICTOR: Leave everything to me.

HARPER: Jack, you'd better wash the car.

JACK: Hang on! (*Whips off his chef's hat and dons his chauffeur's cap.*) You were saying...?

HARPER: Wash the car! You're taking the girls window-shopping.

JACK: The car. Hmm. The car's in no fit state to take anyone anywhere. She's virtually a write-off. It'd break your heart to see her. She's a shadow of her former self. Ha! Ha! Ha! Get it? A *shadow* of her former self? Silver shadow... oh, never mind.

HARPER: Well it's time I had some use out of her.

JACK: Then you shouldn't neglect her, sir. I feel her chugging along on her last legs, and it makes me want to weep. I love that old girl, sir, I really do. There've been times when I've saved money out of my own wages to get her repaired.

HARPER: She can manage a short spin, surely?

JACK: I daren't risk it, sir. I'd never forgive myself if I pushed her too far. She couldn't make it on her own, let alone with three passengers.

VICTOR: Sir, the neighbour's man'll drive them. He can help get dinner ready too.

JACK: Suits me. If she's going to be finished off, I'd rather someone else did it.

VICTOR: Disputatious so and so, isn't he?

JACK: Interfering little goody two shoes, isn't he?

HARPER: Now, now, you two.

JACK: Sir, I can't stand the way he sucks up to you. I know why he rations everything – the food; the wine; the hot water – he's worming his way into your good books. It makes me mad. And then I hear people maligning you every day. It hurts. I care about you, you see, in spite of the way you treat me. You mean more to me than anything in the world, apart from the car. It's really wounding when people call you a miserable, cheese-paring tosser, or a penny-pinching, parsimonious prat, or a scroogy old scumbag, or a mean, morose, decrepit...

HARPER: Do you mind?!

JACK: There's hundreds of stories about you, you know – in the neighbourhood – it's a favourite pass-time.

HARPER: So bloody what? (*Beat.*) Stories? What stories?

JACK: Well, for example, they say you deliberately quarrel with everyone at Christmas so you don't have to give them presents. Then there's a story that you once tried to take the neighbour's dog to court for stealing a sausage. There's even a rumour that you once had a trifle scraped off the kitchen floor and served up to the Chairman of the Conservative Party. It's terrible, sir. You're becoming a by-word.

HARPER: You're a fool. How dare you talk to me like this?

JACK: It's not me that says it, sir.

(*HARPER gives JACK a clip round the ear, then skulks off, then comes back.*)

HARPER: I'm docking your wages for this.

(*He pauses, belts him again round the other ear, and skulks off. VICTOR is laughing.*)

VICTOR: Tough cheese, mate. Looks as though honesty just doesn't pay.

JACK: You stay out of this, Mr Johnny-Come-Lately. Really fancy yourself, don't you. Well, you won't be sniggering when he clobbers *you.*

VICTOR: Hey, cool it, Jack, old son! No sense getting into a state.

JACK: (*Aside.*) He's backtracking. I'll act tough. If he's stupid enough to get scared, I'll belt him one. (*Aloud.*) Look here, you little joker – your jokes aren't funny, right? You get me riled and you'll be laughing on the other side of your face.

41

(Menacingly, JACK pushes VICTOR to the edge of the stage, fists at the ready.)

VICTOR: Oi! There's no call for violence.

JACK: Yes there bloody well *is!*

VICTOR: Please...!

JACK: You jumped-up little squirt!

VICTOR: But, Jack...!

JACK: I'm not Jack to you – not now, slimeball! I've got an old billiard cue upstairs somewhere, and by God if I find it...

VICTOR: A billiard cue, eh?

(VICTOR pushes JACK right back.)

JACK: Billiard cue? Billiard cue? Who said anything about a billiard-cue?

VICTOR: Look here, fathead, if anyone's doing any beating up round here, it's gonna be *me* – got it?

JACK: Anything you say!

VICTOR: A lousy, two-bit cook is what *you* are!

JACK: I know! I know!

VICTOR: And you don't know who *I* am, do you?

JACK: I'm sorry?

VICTOR: You threatened to beat me up.

JACK: It was a joke.

VICTOR: Joke schmoke! I didn't find it funny. *(He lands a punch on JACK and goes.)*

JACK: To hell with honesty! He's right: it *doesn't* pay. I'll never tell the truth again as long as I live. And I'll tell you something else: it's all very well for Mr Harper to go around belting people up, but that little upstart is going to pay for this.

(Enter FAY and MARIANNE.)

FAY: Hello, Jack. Is his lordship in?

JACK: Yes – more's the pity.

FAY: Tell him we're here, would you?

(JACK goes out.)

MARIANNE: Oh, Fay, I'm in such a state! God, but I'm not half dreading this encounter!

FAY: Why? What's there to be alarmed about?

MARIANNE: How can you ask? This is the monster I'm about to marry.

FAY: He's not the ideal husband, I know. You're thinking about that boyfriend of yours, aren't you? The one you were telling me about. It's written all over your face.

MARIANNE: Then how can I deny it? He's called on us a few times – you should see him, Fay – so poised, so charming. He's... made quite an impression on me.

FAY: You mean you want to shag the pants off him.

MARIANNE: Since you put it that way – yes.

FAY: But who is he?

MARIANNE: I've no idea. He's just incredibly sexy. If it was up to me, I'd marry him like a shot. He's the main reason why the idea of Mr Harper fills me with horror.

FAY: These youngsters are fine as far as they go, but most of them are as poor as church-mice. You'll be better off with an old husband who'll leave you lots of money. It won't be too pleasant in the bedroom, I admit. But it won't last long, and believe me, once he's dead you'll be well placed to find yourself a real dish, who'll make up for all the nastiness you went through.

MARIANNE: Things have come to a pretty pass if someone has to die for me to be happy. Besides, Death doesn't necessarily fall in with our plans.

FAY: Don't be silly! You're only marrying him on condition that he leaves you a widow soon. It'll be a downright liberty if he lasts three months. Talk of the devil...

MARIANNE: Oh, Fay, what a dog!

(*Enter HARPER.*)

HARPER: I put my glasses on, my darling. I hope you don't mind. I'd still see how lovely you are without them, but then people look at the stars through lenses, and a star is what you are. The loveliest star in the firmament. Fay, she's not answering. She doesn't seem at all pleased to see me.

FAY: She's stunned. You've bowled her over. And then, girls are always shy about showing what they feel.

HARPER: True. Look, sweet! My daughter's come to say hello.

(*Enter ELEANOR.*)

MARIANNE: (*To ELEANOR.*) I'm afraid this visit's long overdue.

ELEANOR: Nonsense. *I* should have called on *you.*

HARPER: (*To MARIANNE.*) Tall isn't she? Like an overgrown weed.

MARIANNE: (*In a low voice to FAY.*) He's revolting! Oh, Jesus, I'm so *miserable!*

HARPER: What says my love?

FAY: She says she finds you irresistible.

HARPER: You certainly know what to say, you... you luscious little lambchop, you!

MARIANNE: (*Aside.*) He's a monster!

HARPER: What was that?

FAY: You're the one, sir.

HARPER: I'm so glad she likes me.

MARIANNE: (*Aside.*) I can't bear this.

HARPER: Look. Here comes my son as well, to welcome you. (*Enter CHARLIE.*)

MARIANNE: (*Aside to FAY.*) My God! Fay! That's the boy I was telling you about!

FAY: Fancy seeing him here!

MARIANNE: Christ! What am I going to do?

HARPER: (*To MARIANNE.*) You're a bit flummoxed because my children are so old, but don't worry – I'll soon be rid of them.

CHARLIE: (*To MARIANNE.*) To be quite frank, I didn't anticipate this. I was, to say the least, surprised when my father told me about his marriage plans.

MARIANNE: I'm surprised too. I didn't expect this meeting.

CHARLIE: Admittedly, my father couldn't have chosen better, and I'm delighted to have this opportunity of seeing you. That said, I can't pretend to be overjoyed that you're going to be my stepmother. I couldn't bring myself to say that, I'm afraid. I do *not* want you as a *stepmother.* Certain parties may feel I'm being unfriendly, but I know you'll take it in good part. You surely understand that the whole idea of this marriage is repugnant to me. You see the position I'm in, and that my interests can only suffer by it. You won't mind my saying – Father, don't get angry – that if it was up to me, this marriage wouldn't go ahead.

HARPER: (*In a low voice to CHARLIE.*) What kind of compliment is that, you insolent little...?

MARIANNE: For my part, all I can say is: I feel exactly the same way. If you find the idea of my being your stepmother repugnant, I'm just as revolted by the idea of your being my stepson. Please don't think I *want* to put you through this misery. The last thing I wish to do is upset you. I promise you, if I had any choice in the matter, I wouldn't agree to a marriage that distresses you.

HARPER: Ooh! Nice one, darling! Rudeness deserves rudeness. Please excuse my son's manners, my pet. He's an immature idiot. He says these things, and he hasn't the foggiest idea what effect they'll have.

MARIANNE: I assure you, he hasn't offended me in the least. On the contrary, I'm delighted that he's told me just how he feels. I'd have liked him less if he hadn't.

HARPER: It's very good of you to overlook his bolshiness like this. He'll mellow with time. He'll come round to the idea – you'll see.

CHARLIE: No I won't, Father. I can't. (*To MARIANNE.*) You'd better believe that *now*.

HARPER: You impudent little shit!

CHARLIE: You want me to deny my true feelings?

HARPER: Will you kindly change your tune?

CHARLIE: All right. (*To MARIANNE.*) I'll take my father's place, then, if I may. I've never met a girl as delightful as you. Nothing could make me happier than to be loved by you. I'd rather be your husband than the richest tycoon in the world. I'd be honoured! I'd be in a state of grace! To possess you is my sole aim in life. I'd do anything to pull off a coup like that. Nothing and no one could stand in my way.

HARPER: Hey! Steady!

CHARLIE: I was only complimenting her on your behalf.

HARPER: I've got a tongue in my head. I can pay my own compliments. I don't need *you* for a go-between. (*To MARIANNE.*) Dearest, there's no lunch, I fear. I... er... I assumed you'd already eaten.

CHARLIE: Ah, but *I* didn't. I sent out to Selfridges. You name it, I ordered it: I've got some sushi that's to die for, heaps of dim sum; four bottles of 1963 Dom Perignon, and an Anton Mossiman tarte tatin, Oh, and I couldn't resist some of their foie gras – apparently it arrived from Toulouse this morning.

HARPER: YOU DID WHAT?

CHARLIE: I hope it's not too eclectic a selection. I had them charge it all to your account. I hope you don't mind.

HARPER: Too eclectic? TOO ECLECTIC! (*In a low voice to VICTOR.*) Victor, what's going on?

VICTOR: (*In a low voice to HARPER.*) He's off his trolley!

CHARLIE: Is something wrong? Didn't I get enough? Forgive me, Marianne. May I call you Marianne?

MARIANNE: There was no need to get anything – really. Not on *my* account.

ELEANOR: (*Sarcasm.*) Are you sure there's time for lunch? What about our little spree? All those wonderful, expensive things we could be buying.

CHARLIE: (*To MARIANNE.*) What do you think of that diamond ring on my father's finger? Superb, isn't it?

MARIANNE: It's gorgeous.

(*CHARLIE wrenches the ring off HARPER's finger and hands it to MARIANNE.*)

HARPER: But that... that's... what the...?!

CHARLIE: Take a closer look.

MARIANNE: (*Examining it politely, not eagerly.*) Really magnificent.

CHARLIE: He wants you to have it. It was meant to be a surprise, but I couldn't resist telling you.

MARIANNE: But – I couldn't possibly...

(*MARIANNE wants to give the ring back to HARPER. CHARLIE stands in her way.*)

CHARLIE: *No* you don't! It's a present – from him. (*Takes the ring and puts it tenderly on her finger.*) There, look: it was *made* for you.

HARPER: (*Bottled fury, menacing.*) Look here, boy...

CHARLIE: But, Father, surely you want her to keep it – as a token of your love?

HARPER: (A*side, to CHARLIE.*) What the hell do you think you're playing at?! That ring's worth at least... That is, it was your mother's. It's a family heirloom.

CHARLIE: Heirloom schmeirloom – she must have it.

HARPER: Look here, you: it belonged... it belonged to dear Margaret. It reminds me of her whenever I'm checking my... whenever I look at it. Honestly, Charlie, how *could* you? Have you no feelings? You know what she meant to me.

CHARLIE: Isn't he an old sweetie?! He's crying because he thinks you don't want it!

MARIANNE: But I *don't* want it.

CHARLIE: He won't take it back.

HARPER: (*Aside.*) This is intolerable!

MARIANNE: It'd be...

(*CHARLIE continues to stop her returning the ring.*)

CHARLIE: You mustn't return it: you'll hurt his feelings.

MARIANNE: Please...

CHARLIE: No you don't.

HARPER: (*Aside.*) God, I hate him!

CHARLIE: See? He's furious because you won't take it.

HARPER: (*Under breath to CHARLIE.*) You treacherous bastard!

CHARLIE: He's beside himself, look.

HARPER: (*As above, but even more menacing.*) I'll kill you for this!

CHARLIE: Why? I'm doing my best to make her keep it!

HARPER: (*As above.*) Just you wait...!

CHARLIE: He's angry with me now, and it's all your fault.

HARPER: (*As above.*) SWINE!!

CHARLIE: He'll get ill if he goes on like this. Please – say you'll take it.

FAY: Jesus, girl, why so coy? Take the thing if he wants you to.

MARIANNE: (*To HARPER.*) I'll give it back some other time.

(*Enter CLAUDE.*)

CLAUDE: Sir, there's a man in the hall wants to talk to you.

HARPER: Tell him I'm busy. He'd better come back later.

CLAUDE: He says he's got some money for you.

HARPER: (*To MARIANNE.*) I'll be back in a minute. (*Goes.*)
CHARLIE: Meanwhile, let's eat. I'll have it all brought out
to us in the garden.
(*CHARLIE leads MARIANNE, ELEANOR and FAY out.*)
HARPER: (*Returning with an old briefcase.*) Victor, keep an
eye on things. Save as much as you can. You never know,
the shop might take it back.
VICTOR: Consider it done, sir.
(*VICTOR goes, as do CLAUDE and MERVIN.*)
HARPER: That son of mine! He's going to ruin me!
(*HARPER goes out.*)

End of Act Three.

ACT FOUR

CHARLIE, MARIANNE, ELEANOR, FAY.

CHARLIE: Let's go in here. It's much safer. There's no one around. We can speak freely.

ELEANOR: (*To MARIANNE.*) Charlie's told me how much he loves you. I'm in the same boat myself, I'll do everything I can to help you.

MARIANNE: That's a great comfort. I hope you'll always feel like that towards me. Disasters like this won't seem nearly so bad.

FAY: (*To CHARLIE and MARIANNE.*) I'm very angry with you both! You should have told me how serious you were about one another. It would have saved you all this heart-ache. I'd never have let things go this far.

CHARLIE: Don't blame *me!* There's a curse on me. (*To MARIANNE.*) What are *you* going to do?

MARIANNE: Do? What's best for Mummy – that's what I *have* to do.

CHARLIE: That's it, eh? What about what's best for *me?*

MARIANNE: What can I say? My hands are tied. *You'll* have to come up with something.

CHARLIE: You're so helpful!

MARIANNE: What do you want from me? I *have* to think of Mummy. If she wants me to marry your father, then that's what I shall do. It's up to you, Charlie. You'll have to charm her. Make her like you. That's the easiest way to solve the problem, surely? If she likes you and sees how much we're in love... She's not a monster, you know. Far from it, she's the kindest, sweetest soul. She wouldn't be asking me to do this if the situation weren't so desperate. Just be yourself – she'll fall for you – I did, didn't I? And meanwhile, I'll tell her exactly how I feel about you.

CHARLIE: Fay, is there nothing *you* can do?

FAY: I'll try my best. *You* know *me* – I'm an old softy at heart. I'd go out of my way to smooth the course of true love.

MARIANNE: But what *can* you do?

FAY: I'll make her see what you mean to one another.

CHARLIE: This is more like it. I'll charm the old girl, all right. Just you watch me! (*To MARIANNE.*) But you must do your bit. Tell her how wonderful I am. She dotes on you. You can twist her round your little finger if you want to.

MARIANNE: I'll try.

FAY: (*Looks at her watch.*) Pollocks!

MARIANNE: Pardon?

FAY: Pollocks! I'm meeting a friend at the Jackson Pollock exhibition in half an hour. I must fly. Catch you later then. And don't despair: it'll all turn out just fine in the end.

MARIANNE: If you say so.

(*FAY goes.*)

CHARLIE: I'm feeling a bit more optimistic.

MARIANNE: Oh, God, Charlie, I hope she's right.

(*She throws herself into his arms. A steamy embrace. Enter HARPER.*)

HARPER: (*Aside.*) What's this, what's this?! He's snogging her! I smell a rat. (*Aloud.*) The car's ready. You can set out whenever you like.

CHARLIE: Since you're not going with them, I thought *I* would.

HARPER: No. You stay here. They'll be fine on their own, and I need to talk to you.

(*ELEANOR and MARIANNE go.*)

HARPER: Now, my boy: she's going to be your stepmother, I know, but leaving that aside, what do you make of her?

CHARLIE: What do I make of her?

HARPER: Yes. Her figure. Her face. Her manner. Her mind.

CHARLIE: She'll do.

HARPER: She'll do?

CHARLIE: To be honest, I was rather disappointed. She's a bit of a frump. Her face is nothing to write home about. She's shamelessly flirtatious. And her mind's as hum-drum as they come. But don't think I'm trying to put you off her. As stepmothers go, she'll do as well as the next.

HARPER: But about ten minutes ago you said to her...

CHARLIE: I was flattering her on your behalf – to please you.

HARPER: Then you don't fancy her?

CHARLIE: You must be joking!

HARPER: Too bad. That puts paid to a scheme I'd just cooked up. Seeing the girl made me worry about my age. People might criticise me for marrying such a young thing. I'd decided to give up the idea. If you hadn't taken a dislike to her, I might have let you have her.

CHARLIE: Really?

HARPER: Really.

CHARLIE: Look: she's not my type, it's true, but I could see my way to marrying her – to please you.

HARPER: You must think I'm a real brute! Of course I wouldn't dream of trying to force her on you. Besides, as your sister keeps pointing out, I've no legal right to.

CHARLIE: Don't worry – I could endure a lot to please you.

HARPER: (*Under breath.*) To get your hands on that trust fund, you mean. (*Aloud.*) Oh, no – that's no recipe for a happy marriage.

CHARLIE: Happiness might come with time. People often marry first and fall in love later.

HARPER: I won't hear of it. It's too risky. Who knows what disasters might ensue. Divorce proceedings – legal fees – alimony – expense, expense, always expense! If you'd taken the tiniest shine to her, it would have been a different story. As it is, I suppose I'd better proceed with plan A.

CHARLIE: You mean...?

HARPER: That's right: marry her myself.

CHARLIE: I can see I'm going to have to tell you everything. I'm in love with her. I have been for several months. But when you told me you wanted to marry her yourself – well...

HARPER: Have you been... seeing her?

CHARLIE: I have.

HARPER: A lot of her?

CHARLIE: Quite a lot.

HARPER: All of her?

CHARLIE: Father, please!

HARPER: And how does she feel about *you?*

CHARLIE: She loves me. But she didn't know I was your son. That's why she was so horrif... so surprised just now.

HARPER: And she knows you want to marry her?

CHARLIE: Absolutely. Her mother knows a bit about us too.

HARPER: I'm glad you've let me into the secret. Well, son, you're going to have to give her up.

CHARLIE: I'll do no such thing! I'll fight you for her tooth and nail. Her mother may be on your side, but *love's* on *mine.*

HARPER: How dare you queer my pitch like this, you treacherous toad?!

CHARLIE: *I'm* queering *your* pitch! Ha! Who saw her first, you lecherous old lammergeyer?

HARPER: I'm your father. I demand respect... You won't get a penny of your precious trust fund – not while I'm around.

CHARLIE: Sod the trust fund. I'll marry her anyway. I love her. And she loves me.

HARPER: Her mother has other ideas though, doesn't she? And from what I hear, Marianne'll do what she's told – unlike some offspring I could name.

CHARLIE: You can threaten me till the cows come home. It won't make a scrap of difference.

HARPER: You're to give her up, do you hear? I'll cut you off without a penny...

CHARLIE: Go ahead!

HARPER: I'll teach you to cross swords with *me!*
(*Enter JACK.*)

HARPER: Ah! Jack! Just the man! Haven't you got a billiard cue somewhere? I think I've just found a use for it.

JACK: (*To HARPER.*) What's going on, sir? Are you two quarrelling again?

CHARLIE: (*To HARPER.*) You're pathetic – you know that? Absolutely pathetic!

JACK: (*To CHARLIE.*) Now now, sir.

HARPER: (*To CHARLIE.*) You just don't think about my feelings, do you? Have you any idea how hurtful all this is? What do you think your mother'd say? (*Produces a photo and gazes at it tearfully.*) Eh? Just look at her. Just look at those kind, gentle eyes, imploring you to show your poor old father a bit of respect. (*Produces a handkerchief and blows his nose histrionically.*)

JACK: (*To HARPER.*) Now now, sir, don't go upsetting yourself.

CHARLIE: I won't budge an inch.

JACK: Is that any way to talk to your father?

HARPER: It's all right, Jack – I can handle him.

JACK: But billiard-cues, sir? Really! He may be a bit of a handful at times, but he's still your son.

HARPER: All right, I tell you what: why don't you act as arbitrator? Then we'll know for certain that I'm in the right.

JACK: Arbitrator, eh? All right. Master Charlie, move off a little way, if you wouldn't mind.

(*CHARLIE goes to the other side of the stage.*)

HARPER: Okay: I'm in love with this girl. I want to marry her. And that little sh- (*JACK puts a finger to his lips.*) that little shyster over there has the audacity to be in love with her too. What's more, he won't give her up when I tell him to.

JACK: He's in the wrong.

HARPER: I ask you, Jack – after all I've done for him! Isn't it atrocious? Should a son fight with his own father? Doesn't the little ponce owe me at least a modicum of respect? Enough to stop him trespassing on *my* territory, at any rate?

JACK: I couldn't agree more, sir. Let me speak to him. Wait there.

(*JACK goes over to CHARLIE.*)

JACK: Well?

CHARLIE: It's like this: I'm in love with this girl. She loves me. Then my father goes and sticks his oar in. Wants to marry her himself.

JACK: He's in the wrong – definitely.

CHARLIE: He should be ashamed of himself! She's young enough to be his granddaughter! I mean, the idea of him still wanting sex! It's disgusting! Shouldn't he leave that to the young?

JACK: You're right. He's crazy. Let me have a word with him. (*He goes back to HARPER.*) Well, your son's not as difficult as you think: he's listening to reason. He's says he's cooled down a bit now; he knows he should respect you and he's ready to go along with whatever you wish, as long as *you're* prepared to treat him better in future.

HARPER: Tell him: in that case I'll give him whatever he wants.

JACK: Will do. (*Going over to CHARLIE.*) Well, your father's not as unreasonable as you make out. He says he only got angry because *you* were out of order, and because you carry on the way you do. Provided you behave in future, and show him the proper respect, you can have whatever you want.

CHARLIE: Jack, you can tell him, as long as he consents to my marrying Marianne, I'll be as good as gold. I'll never step out of line again.

JACK: (*Going back to HARPER.*) It's a done deal. He'll do as you ask.

HARPER: Excellent!

JACK: (*Going back to CHARLIE.*) Success. You've given him your word, and he's happy.

CHARLIE: Thank God!

JACK: Gentlemen, you can talk things over now. You're in agreement. It was a what-ye-call-it? – a breakdown of communication, that's all.

CHARLIE: Jack, I'll be indebted to you for the rest of my life.

JACK: It was nothing, sir.

HARPER: (*To JACK.*) You've done me a great service, and you deserve some reward. (*He puts his hand in his trouser pocket, giving JACK the momentary idea that he's going to produce a gratuity – then wipes his brow with it.*) I'll bear it in mind, I promise. Off you go now.

JACK: Tata. (*He goes.*)

CHARLIE: I'm sorry if I got carried away.

HARPER: Forget it.

CHARLIE: No, really, I'll find it hard to forgive myself.

HARPER: I'm delighted that you've come to your senses.

CHARLIE: So you're ready to let bygones be bygones – so soon? What a sweetie!

HARPER: It's easy to forgive your children when they come to heel.

CHARLIE: What about all my extravagances? The Oxfam shop? You're really not angry any more?

HARPER: How could I be, now you're so obedient and respectful?

CHARLIE: You're so good to me. I'll never forget this as long as I live, I promise you.

HARPER: And *I* promise *you* I'll give you anything you want.

CHARLIE: I want nothing – now you've given me Marianne.

HARPER: Who said I'd done that?

CHARLIE: You.

HARPER: Me?!

CHARLIE: Of course.

HARPER: What do you mean? *You* just agreed to give her up.

CHARLIE: Give her up?!

HARPER: Yes.

CHARLIE: I did no such thing.

HARPER: Oh?

CHARLIE: On the contrary, I'm more hellbent on having her than ever.

HARPER: Why you… you duplicitous cur!

CHARLIE: My mind's made up.

HARPER: I'll soon change it for you, you miserable lump of dung!

CHARLIE: Go ahead and try!

HARPER: I never want to clap eyes on you again!

CHARLIE: Fine!

HARPER: I disown you!

CHARLIE: See if I care!

HARPER: I'm cutting you off!

CHARLIE: Go ahead!

HARPER: My curse – that's all you're getting out of me!

CHARLIE: You're too kind!

(*HARPER goes. Enter FLETCHER, from the garden, carrying a bulging briefcase.*)

FLETCHER: Ah, Charlie. Just the man I was looking for. Come with me – now!

CHARLIE: What is it?

FLETCHER: Just come with me! We're in clover.

CHARLIE: We are?

FLETCHER: I've had my beady eye on this all day.

CHARLIE: What is it?

FLETCHER: Your father's money.

CHARLIE: How did you get hold of it?

FLETCHER: I'll tell you later. We're out of here! That's him yelling now.

(*They go. HARPER enters from the garden, bellowing.*)

HARPER: Stop thief!! Murder!! Rape!! Help!! I'm ruined!! I demand justice!! Someone's stolen my money! He might has well have cut my throat. Where is he? *Who* is he? (*Catching hold of himself.*) Got him! Shit! It's me! I'm so depressed! I hardly know who I am. Oh my God! My beloved money! Where are you? You were my North and South, my East and West, My working day and my Sunday rest, My noon, my midnight, my talk, my song... oh, fucking *hell!* How can I survive without you? I'm all washed up! Dead and buried! Resurrect me, somebody! Give me back my dosh, or tell me who took it! Eh? What was that? Nothing. Whoever did it must have been biding their time. They swiped it while I was talking to that wretched son of mine. I'm fetching the police. I'm going to have the entire household interrogated. (*Sees audience.*) Who are all these people?! (*Peering at them.*) I suspect you – all of you! What was that? What did you say? Something about the thief? Is he out there, then? I beg of you, if anyone knows anything about this, will they please tell me. Is he hiding out there? (*To himself again.*) They're all looking at me – *laughing* at me! It's a conspiracy, and they're all in it! Fetch the police, someone! Fetch the magistrates! The judges! The jury! The Prime Minister! The European army! If I don't get my money back I'll have everyone hanged, and then I'll hang *myself!*

End of Act Four.

56

ACT FIVE

HARPER, DETECTIVE.

DETECTIVE: I'll take care of everything, sir. I've been solving robberies like this for years. If I could have a thousand quid for every thief I've caught…

HARPER: If I don't get my money back I'm taking this to the highest court in the land.

DETECTIVE: We must do everything by the book. Now then: exactly how much money was there in this briefcase?

HARPER: Ninety-eight thousand, two hundred and fifty-five pounds and seventy-two p.

DETECTIVE: In a single briefcase? You're mad!

HARPER: Don't you start.

DETECTIVE: Hmm… (*Noting it down on a small jotting pad.*) That's quite a robbery!

HARPER: No punishment could be severe enough. If this bastard goes free, it'll be the end of civilisation as we know it.

DETECTIVE: What was the money in?

HARPER: I told you, a briefcase.

DETECTIVE: (*Impatient.*) What *denominations?*

HARPER: Hundred pound notes, most of it.

DETECTIVE: Any suspects?

HARPER: Yes. Everyone. Round up the whole neighbourhood.

DETECTIVE: We must tread carefully. We don't want to scare the thief off. We'll garner our clues first, and then we'll pounce. You'll get your money back.
(*Enter JACK.*)

JACK: (*Talking to someone off.*) I won't be a minute. Just chop his feet off, could you, and dump him in boiling water. Then hang him from the ceiling for an hour or two.

HARPER: Who? The thief?

JACK: No, sir. A suckling pig. Harrods just sent it round.

HARPER: (*Choking.*) Harrods!!!

JACK: Would you have preferred Fortnums, sir?

57

(*A glare from HARPER.*)

JACK: I'm doing you *cochon de lait à la Jack.*

HARPER: Never mind that now. You've got to talk to the inspector here.

DETECTIVE: There's no cause for alarm, sir. I won't make things hard for you.

JACK: (*To HARPER.*) Will he be joining you for dinner, sir?

DETECTIVE: Are you evading the issue?

JACK: Excuse me! I don't call a suckling pig evading the issue.

HARPER: That's not what we're talking about.

JACK: If things aren't up to the mark, you can blame that bloody Victor. He doesn't give me a chance with his wretched economies.

HARPER: You know damned well we're not talking about the sodding dinner, you treacherous, two-faced worm! What do you know about the money that's been stolen from me?

JACK: Money? Stolen?

HARPER: Yes, scum, and *you* stole it! If you don't give it back I'll throttle you with my bare hands.

DETECTIVE: Oh, we won't be needing an interrogation. He looks like an honest man to me. He'll tell us everything we need to know. (*To JACK.*) Just you spit it all out and you won't come to any harm. And I dare say your master'll give you a suitable reward. He had a briefcase stolen earlier today. You wouldn't happen to know anything about it?

JACK: (*Aside.*) Here's my chance to get my own back on that swine, Victor. He's ruled the roost round here since he arrived. *And* he beat me up. I won't forget *that* in a hurry.

HARPER: What are you mumbling about?

DETECTIVE: Leave him be. He's probably working out his statement.

JACK: (*To HARPER.*) You want the truth, sir? It was Victor.

HARPER: Victor?!

JACK: Yes.

HARPER: And I thought he was so loyal.

JACK: Well, *he* took the money.

DETECTIVE: What's your reason for thinking that?

JACK: My reason?

DETECTIVE: Hm.

JACK: I just know.

DETECTIVE: But you must have some sort of proof.

HARPER: Did you see him snooping about in the garden, for instance?

JACK: Oh, sure. Snooping about like nobody's business, he was. What was it in, this money?

HARPER: A briefcase.

JACK: That settles it: I saw him with a briefcase.

HARPER: Describe it.

JACK: Describe it?

HARPER: Describe it.

JACK: It looked like – like... well, exactly like a briefcase, really.

HARPER: You don't say!

DETECTIVE: Go on...

JACK: Weeell... it was quite a *small* briefcase.

HARPER: Can't have been mine then. Mine was medium-sized.

JACK: What I mean is, *relatively speaking*. It was small *relative* to a really enormous briefcase.

DETECTIVE: What colour was it?

JACK: What colour?

DETECTIVE: What colour?

JACK: What colour... what colour... what colour would *you* say it was?

HARPER: Oh, for God's sake, Jack!

JACK: It was a sort of... briefcasey colour.

DETECTIVE: Can you be a little more specific?

JACK: (*Plumping desperately.*) Red... I think.

HARPER: Mine was grey.

JACK: Exactly! It was a sort of reddish-grey.

HARPER: That's it then. Victor's the thief. (*To DETECTIVE.*) Take his statement. I don't know! You can't trust anyone. I'll be robbing *myself* next!

JACK: Sir, here he comes. Don't tell him it was me that ratted on him.

(Enter VICTOR.)

HARPER: Come and confess your crime, you thieving bastard!

VICTOR: Is something wrong, sir?

HARPER: You have the gall to try and brazen it out?

VICTOR: 'Confess your crime' you said – what crime?

HARPER: You know damned well what crime, you little hypocrite. It's no use pretending. I've heard the whole story. How could you do this to me, after I took you in, gave you a job, food, clothing, shelter...! I've clutched a viper to my very bosom! You've broken my heart!

VICTOR: Since you know the truth, sir, I'll be completely straight with you.

JACK: *(Aside.)* Jesus! I flushed him out by accident!

VICTOR: I was waiting for the right moment to tell you. But since it's panned out like this, please don't lose your temper – let me explain.

HARPER: Explain?! You've taken from me what I hold most dear!

VICTOR: Sir, I've done you wrong, I know. But is it really such a grave offence?

HARPER: Of course it's grave. You might as well have killed me.

VICTOR: Please keep calm, sir, and hear my side of it.

HARPER: You rob me of my life-blood; rip out my entrails; and then try to defend yourself!

VICTOR: Your entrails are in good hands – if I can put it like that. I'm well-connected; my father's rich; *(Temptingly.)* I can easily... make amends.

HARPER: You're damned right you'll make amends! You'll give me back what you've taken. What you've done – it's worse than rape.

VICTOR: Oh, nothing... of *that* nature has happened. Nor will it.

HARPER: What do you mean, nothing of that nature? Just tell me: what on earth induced you to do this?

VICTOR: Can't you guess?

HARPER: No.

VICTOR: Love. What else?

HARPER: Love?

VICTOR: Yes.

HARPER: So you love my money?

VICTOR: Of course not. Just let me keep what I've got, and I'll ask for nothing more – not one penny.

HARPER: You must be joking! I've never heard such an outrageous suggestion. To commit a robbery and then try to hang on to the loot!

VICTOR: You call it a robbery?

HARPER: What else am I supposed to call it? A haul like that.

VICTOR: I agree – it *is* quite a haul. I couldn't have done better. But you haven't really lost it – just entrusted it to me. Do the right thing – let me keep it.

HARPER: LET YOU KEEP IT!! CHRIST!!!

VICTOR: You'll have to kill me if you want it back.

HARPER: He's obsessed with my money!

VICTOR: I've already told you: this isn't about financial gain. How could you impute such sordid motives to me?

HARPER: Oh! Oh, I see! So you're going to start a charity! That's all right, then! (*Beat.*) Over my dead body! I'll make you pay for this, if there's any justice in the land.

VICTOR: You must act as you think fit. Only, promise you won't drag Eleanor into this. She's entirely innocent.

HARPER: I should hope so too! Where *is* the haul, though? I want to see it. Where have you hidden it?

VICTOR: The 'haul' is in the house. Why would I want to hide it anywhere?

HARPER: And you haven't meddled with it?

VICTOR: I already said, it's not *like* that. My intentions are entirely honourable.

HARPER: Honourable! Ha!

VICTOR: Your suspicions are unfair to both of us. If you knew the kind of adoration I feel – so intense and yet so pure...

HARPER: Adoration, he calls it!

VICTOR: I'd rather die than overstep the mark. I've restrained my... baser urges, despite all that loveliness.

HARPER: Baser urges? Loveliness?

VICTOR: Look, don't touch – that's the rule I've followed. I've behaved impeccably. I've been the model lover.

HARPER: He talks about my money as though it were a woman.

VICTOR: Sir, your daughter…

HARPER: Eleanor again. Where the hell does *she* come into it?

VICTOR: We're engaged.

HARPER: WHAT??!! First he steals my money – then my daughter!

JACK: (*To DETECTIVE.*) I hope you're taking this down.

HARPER: (*To DETECTIVE.*) He's a robber *and* a rapist. How many years will he get?

VICTOR: How dare you call me that?! When you find out who I am…

(*Enter ELEANOR, MARIANNE, FAY.*)

HARPER: There you are, you evil creature! You don't deserve a father like me. I thought I'd taught you how to behave. How could you fall for a criminal, let alone get engaged to him? I'll bet you're in it together. Well, you won't get away with it, either of you. (*To ELEANOR.*) I'm placing you under house arrest (*To VICTOR.*) and *you're* going to prison.

VICTOR: You're too upset to make a proper judgement. You must at least hear me out before condemning me.

HARPER: Prison's too lenient. If only they had firing squads in this country.

ELEANOR: Please don't be such a brute. Don't let your temper run away with you. Take your time – think things through. Is there really anything to take offence at? Haven't you blown this out of all proportion? You'd be less horrified by our engagement if you knew that, but for him, you'd have lost me some time ago. You see, he's the one I told you about; the one rescued me – in Verbier – when I fell into that snow drift.

HARPER: So sodding what? I'd rather he'd left you to die than stolen my money. And anyway, what were you doing in Verbier in the first place?

ELEANOR: If you mean the money, my friend paid for me. Oh, Father, I beg of you… if you love me at all…

HARPER: Save your breath. This shyster's going to jail.

JACK: (*To VICTOR.*) This'll teach you to go around beating people up.

FAY: What the hell's going on?

(*Enter SIR ARTHUR EDGERTON.*)

HARPER: Sir Arthur! Am I glad to see you.

SIR ARTHUR: (*To HARPER.*) You seem upset. What's the matter?

HARPER: I'm the wretchedest man on God's earth! The marriage is a non-starter. Robbery! Rape! You name it, we've had it. See that weasel there? He insinuated himself into my nest and sucked my eggs. He got a job as my butler so he could steal my money and violate my child. I ask you!

VICTOR: For the last time, I *haven't* violated her! And what the hell's your money got to do with this?

HARPER: (*To SIR ARTHUR.*) They're engaged. What are you going to do about it? Perhaps we can sue him? A joint action. Could be lucrative. What do you say?

SIR ARTHUR: I've no wish to marry the girl against her will. Besides, I don't imagine for one minute that she'd have me.

HARPER: See that lad there? Detective. Knows his job. (*To DETECTIVE.*) Charge him. And be sure to get every last, sordid detail into your report.

VICTOR: You're mad! I love your daughter. That's not a crime. What's more, when you know who I am you won't...

HARPER: Who you are, indeed! Bullshit! I suppose you're going to try and pass yourself off as some kind of toff. You've got a nerve, you have.

VICTOR: I wouldn't dream of doing such a thing. I've too much integrity. No – just ask anyone in Swanage – they'll vouch for me.

HARPER: Swanage?

SIR ARTHUR: (*To VICTOR.*) You're skating on thin ice, sir. I know Swanage inside out. Strike one false note and I'll detect it.

VICTOR: If you're familiar with the place, you'll have heard of Thomas Alberry.

SIR ARTHUR: Of course. Few people knew him better than I.

HARPER: I don't give a bishop's fart about any Thomas Alberry.

SIR ARTHUR: Please – let's hear what he has to say.

VICTOR: Thomas Alberry was my father.

SIR ARTHUR: He was?!

VICTOR: Yes.

SIR ARTHUR: You're making fun of me. You'd better think up a better story. A lie like that won't save you.

VICTOR: Watch what you say. It's no lie. I can prove it, too – easily.

SIR ARTHUR: What? You dare claim to be Thomas Alberry's son?

VICTOR: Yes. I'll maintain it against all comers.

SIR ARTHUR: You've got quite a nerve – I'll say that for you. Thomas Alberry died years ago. He was killed in a yacht-wreck.

ELEANOR: A what-wreck?

SIR ARTHUR: A yacht-wreck.

HARPER: Whose yacht?

SIR ARTHUR: Mine.

HARPER: Yours?

SIR ARTHUR: Alberry, his wife and their two children drowned during a hurricane in the Caribbean. They were on their way into exile.

ELEANOR: Political?

SIR ARTHUR: No – tax.

HARPER: (*To himself.*) Tax, eh? Hmmmm... (*looking at VICTOR in a new light.*)

VICTOR: (*To SIR ARTHUR.*) But you see, *I survived* the wreck. I somehow lost my memory, though – I suppose a mast or something must have hit me on the head. As far as I *knew*, I wasn't carrying any documents that might have provided a clue to my identity. The helmsman rescued me. Since he and his wife had no children of their own, they decided to adopt me. They behaved towards me exactly like a father and mother. When I got my memory back, and asked them where my real parents were, they told me they'd both drowned. Recently, though, my adopted father died. On his deathbed he confessed to me that he and my adopted mother had deliberately concealed my true identity from me. I'd had my passport on me when he rescued me from the wreck, but he'd kept it hidden away for years. I've been carrying out enquiries about my real parents, as it occurred to me that they might have survived too. But my love for Eleanor kept me from actually going and looking for them.

SIR ARTHUR: Have you still got that passport?

VICTOR: It's with me wherever I go.

SIR ARTHUR: May I see it?

(*VICTOR produces the passport and hands it to SIR ARTHUR. Meanwhile, MARIANNE has clearly been putting two and two together. She rushes over to and looks at the passport over SIR ARTHUR's shoulder.*)

MARIANNE: I don't believe it! It's him!

VICTOR: Who?

MARIANNE: My brother! You're my brother!

VICTOR: But that's incredible!

MARIANNE: Incredible, but true: Mother and I survived the wreck too. We drifted for several days in a rubber dinghy, before we were picked up by another yacht. Its owner was an international criminal with all sorts of interests, including white slaving. We were sold to a German billionaire, who kept us for five years in his mansion in the Black Forest. Eventually we escaped, since when we've been living in Hounslow.

JACK: Hounslow? Jesus!

SIR ARTHUR: This is a miracle – a double miracle – a treble miracle!

VICTOR/MARIANNE: You mean...?

SIR ARTHUR: Yes! I'm your father! Come here, both of you – let me hold you. (*They go to him and all three embrace.*)

MARIANNE: Then it's you my mother's been mourning for all these years!

HARPER: But just now you said you were dead.

SIR ARTHUR: I have to be careful.

HARPER: Tax...?

SIR ARTHUR: Exactly.

(*VICTOR glances uneasily at the DETECTIVE, who gestures indulgence.*)

You see, after the wreck, I couldn't return to England. If I had, I'd have been arrested for tax fraud, and probably imprisoned for several years. Since there was no life for me here, and after failing to trace my wife and children, I decided to start afresh in Switzerland. That was when I changed my name. If I'd stuck with Thomas Alberry, my new business associates might have found out about my past, and I'd have been finished. I missed home, of course, terribly. So would you if you'd lived in Switzerland for any length of time. Eventually my love of my native land proved too strong. Two years ago I decided to risk coming back to Blighty. Still using my new name, I purchased a shell company and transferred all my interests here.

HARPER: So you deal in shells? That doesn't sound very promising. I'd been given to understand that you were some sort of tycoon. I must say, if I'd known this I don't think I'd ever have cultivated your acquaintance.

SIR ARTHUR: You misunderstand me: a shell company is a business term – it means a kind of holding company.

HARPER: A holding company, eh? You mean, with lots of little companies in it?

SIR ARTHUR: That's right.

HARPER: How many little companies?

SIR ARTHUR: A hundred and twenty-two, at the last count. Didn't I tell you that?

HARPER: That sounds a lot healthier... So – what exactly are we saying here? Is this boy your son? (*Points to VICTOR.*)

SIR ARTHUR: He is indeed.

HARPER: Then you owe me more than half a million pounds. He stole them from me.

SIR ARTHUR: He did? I'm sorry to hear that.

VICTOR: (*To HARPER.*) Who told you that?

HARPER: Jack.

VICTOR: (*To JACK.*) You told him that?

JACK: I have the right to remain silent.

HARPER: The detective here took a statement from him.

VICTOR: And do you really think I'm capable of such a thing?

(*Enter CHARLIE.*)

HARPER: I don't care whether you're capable of it or not. I want my money back. NOW!!

CHARLIE: (*To HARPER.*) Relax. I've heard about your little disaster. I want to marry Marianne – right? Just give your consent, and you'll get your money back.

HARPER: Where is it?

CHARLIE: Don't worry about that. I know where it is and I'm in control of the situation. Just come to a decision. You've got a choice: either I marry Marianne, with *your* consent, or you lose your money.

HARPER: You haven't spent any yet?

CHARLIE: Not a penny. Now, *do* we have your blessing? As for Marianne's mother, she's already said that, as far as she's concerned, her daughter's free to marry whoever she wants.

SIR ARTHUR: (*To HARPER.*) Mr Harper, I'm sure you realise that a girl's more likely to choose the son than the father. Give your consent, or something hurtful may be said – something there was no need for you hear, or me, for that matter. Let's have a double wedding. What do you say?

HARPER: Let me see my money. It'll help me make my mind up.

CHARLIE: You'll see it – completely intact.

HARPER: (*To SIR ARTHUR.*) Will you pay for the weddings?

SIR ARTHUR: I will. Happy now?

HARPER: I'd also like a new suit for the occasion – from Savile Row.

SIR ARTHUR: Savile Row it is. Now, let's all try and be *happy*, since this is a happy day.

DETECTIVE: There could well be a fine for wasting police time.

HARPER: We haven't wasted your time. You can get him
  for making a false statement. (*Indicating JACK.*)
JACK: What am I supposed do? I'm beaten up when I tell
  the truth and thrown in jail when I lie.
SIR ARTHUR: Mr Harper... Gerald...
HARPER: Hmmm?
SIR ARTHUR: Gerald, don't press charges, please.
HARPER: Will you pay the fine?
SIR ARTHUR: Gladly.
HARPER: Excellent! That's settled, then.
SIR ARTHUR: A double wedding. How perfectly splendid.
  (*To MARIANNE and VICTOR.*) Let's go and tell your
  mother the good news.
HARPER: And I'll go and check on my money.

The End.

THE IDIOT

Characters

LELIE

MASCARILLE

CELIE

TRUFALDIN

ANSELME

PANDOLFE

HIPPOLYTE

LEANDRE

ERGASTE

ANDRES

ACT ONE

LELIE alone.

LELIE: Léandre, for one heart we both vie –
You love Célie and so do I –
We're victims of the same allure.
Well, we can't *share* her, that's for sure –
We're going to have fight it out.
Your love, or mine, is up the spout.
And let me warn you, here and now:
I mean to win, I don't care how,
It's do or die, the gloves are off,
And *your* gloves I suggest *you* doff.
The die is cast... Ah! Mascarille.
(*Enter MASCARILLE.*)
MASCARILLE: What's up?
LELIE: A fresh catastrophe:
My amorous plans have gone awry
A second blinking time, and why?
Léandre again! He loves Célie!
No sooner have *I* changed, than *he*,
The bloody fool, has followed suit!
It's Hell! My *stars* have brought me to it –
They seem to have it in for me.
MASCARILLE: Léandre loves Célie? I see!
LELIE: He's *hopelessly* in love with her.
MASCARILLE: Oh, dear! That *is* a pity, sir.
LELIE: You can say *that* abloodygain!
I'm in complete *despair.* But then
I shouldn't give up hope just yet –
With you to aid and to abet,
Devise some ruse, or set some snare,
There must be chances, mustn't there?
It's not the nightmare that it seems.
You're *always* thinking up new schemes,
Your ingenuity is rare,
As servants go, beyond compare,

You're probably the cleverest one
In the whole country...
MASCARILLE: Steady on!
I hate you flattering me, sir,
It makes me nervous. I prefer
The insults and the threats I get
When you are angry, or upset.
LELIE: That isn't fair, as well you know.
I'd rather change the subject, though:
My slave girl, my divine Célie –
She's perfect, wouldn't you agree?
She's made to melt the hardest heart –
I really don't know where to start,
Which of her many marvellous traits
Deserves the first and highest praise:
Not only does she *look* sublime,
I keep discovering, all the time,
In chance *remarks* that she lets fall
A *wisdom* that is not at all
Consistent with her lowly rank.
For *that* she has *bad luck* to thank –
Yes, it is *Fate* that's brought her low
And now perversely keeps her so,
Conceals her birth with servile chains.
MASCARILLE: I think love's addling your brains
And planting mad thoughts in your head:
What of your father? He'll see red –
Yes, old Pandolfe – remember him?
He'll tear you limb from stupid limb!
You know how easily he's riled
When you wax whimsical and wild
And give romantic dreams the helm.
He's in discussions with Anselme,
You're marrying his Hippolyte,
That's how your father means to beat
This sort of nonsense out of you –
Believe you me, sir, if he knew
That you'd defied his plans, and strayed,
Fallen for some young scullery-maid

Of unknown origin – oh, dear,
He'd slit your throat from ear to ear,
He'd hang you out to dry, he would –
LELIE: Scaring me won't do any good.
MASCARILLE: Oh? If it makes you change your ways...
LELIE: To rile a master rarely pays –
    It's not the province of valets
    To tell their masters how to live
    And sound off all the time, and give
    Opinions that have not been sought.
MASCARILLE: Don't get all tense and overwrought!
    I was just testing you, monsieur,
    Gauging how strong your feelings were,
    You think I'd take that attitude?
    Since when was Mascarille a prude,
    A killjoy? Eh? Is that my style?
    Of course not, not by many a mile,
    If I've a fault it isn't that
    It's looking too benignly at
    Actions I really should condemn
    And trying to see some good in them –
    I'm *too humane,* I am, by far –
    It's terrible, but there you are,
    What can one do? You father? Pish!
    You do exactly as you wish,
    So he'll pontificate and scream
    And let off his paternal steam,
    To Hell with him! His fire's gone cold,
    He's withered, impotent, and old,
    He's through with pleasures and amours
    So now he tries to stamp on yours,
    He'd sow his oats like billyoh
    If he had any left to sow.
    Na, give your young desires full bent,
    You stray, sir, to your heart's content.
LELIE: Is father *jealous?*
MASCARILLE: Is grass green?
    I'm here, sir, like I've always been –
    I'll help you any way can.

75

LELIE: You *are* the perfect serving man!
    The eyes from which arose my flame
    Now burn themselves.
MASCARILLE: She feels the same?
LELIE: That is precisely what I mean.
    But since *Léandre* is on the scene
    God only knows what might occur:
    He says he's set on having her.
    I'm counting now on your shrewd head –
    I have to put the thing to bed
    Immediately and make her mine
    What ruse, wile, stratagem, design
    Can you devise, at once, to thwart
    My rival?
MESCARILLE: This requires some thought...
    What schemes have I, what scams or tricks
    To extricate you from this fix...?
    (*MASCARILLE thinks.*)
LELIE: Well?... What have you come up with?
MASCARILLE: Here!
    I can't just conjure an idea
    Out of thin air!... You might...
LELIE: Might what?
MASCARILLE: Na... You could...
LELIE: Go on...
MASCARILLE: Maybe not...
    ...Perhaps if you...
LELIE: Perhaps if I...?
MASCARILLE: Na... This one *might* be worth a try...
LELIE: Let's hear it then.
MASCARILLE: (*Shaking his head.*) Na, that won't do.
    There's only one course left to you –
    To tell your father.
LELIE: (*Heavy irony.*) Oh! Oh, right!
    Brilliant!
MASCARILLE: Okay, that's not too bright...
    But you must have her... let me see...
    Trufaldin *owns* her, doesn't he?

LELIE: He does.
MASCARILLE: Then talk to *him* instead.
LELIE: And tell him what?
(*MASCARIILLE shrugs.*)
LELIE: You muttonhead!
Stop dithering. This is not a joke.
MASCARILLE: We'd be all right if *you* weren't broke –
Then you could simply *buy* Célie
And *he'd* be scuppered, wouldn't he?
Some gypsies have been eyeing her –
They're after her – at least they were –
They haven't stumped the cash up yet
And Trufaldin's begun to fret –
If *you* could step in with some gold...
LELIE: You think he'd sell?
MASCARILLE: Is Greenland cold?
Money's his god, he knows no other,
For fifty francs he'd flog his mother.
Yeees, it's a pity you're so skint.
Your father's such an old skinflint
It's no use going to *him* for bread –
The whole thing's hopeless, like I said.
But isn't that Célie's window?
It wouldn't hurt for us to know
How *she* regards the state of play –
Why don't you try and quiz her, eh?
LELIE: Trufaldin guards her night and day.
Watches her like a mean old hawk –
We'll never get a chance to talk.
(*CELIE appears at the window.*)
MASCARILLE: There she is now, look, bang on cue!
For once your stars are helping you.
(*CELIE comes out of the house.*)
LELIE: Célie, oh, empress of my heart!
What is this lapse on Fortune's part?
Such beauty – why does God permit
A wretch like me to gaze on it?
What bliss to see those eyes again
Though all they've given me is pain!

CELIE: Please promise me that isn't true!
I'll tear them out if they've hurt *you!*
LELIE: Not hurt, my love – the pain is bliss!
What should I cherish more than this...
This *glorious* wound, this...!
MASCARILLE: Oh, my gawd!
He's off! (*To LELIE.*) Monsieur, you can't afford
To waste the time with talk like this –
Say what the situation is
And ask her how she thinks...
TRUFALDIN: (*From within.*)   Célie-eee!
LELIE: And now my stars are thwarting me!
I bet that's bloody Trufaldin,
The nasty, nosy little man!
MASCARILLE: Monsieur, you'd better disappear –
Be off with you – and have no fear
I'll find out what she thinks – somehow.
(*TRUFALDIN comes out of the house.*)
TRUFALDIN: (*To CELIE.*) Who were you talking to just now?
Were you accosting passers by?
I did forbid that, didn't I?
CELIE: But this was somebody I knew.
A sweet boy, and a good one, too.
TRUFALDIN: Oh, yes?
CELIE: (*Sourly.*)   His morals have been checked –
He's nobody you need suspect.
MASCARILLE: Is Monsieur Trufaldin in there?
Monsieur, allow me to declare
How honoured, *overjoyed* I am
To speak to such a... *famous* man.
TRUFALDIN: (*Coming out.*) What? Famous? Me?
MASCARILLE: This lady, sir –
Her mystic skills have caused a stir –
She prophesies the future, no?
At least, my sources tell me so.
I need to speak with her.
TRUFALDIN: Oh, yes?
(*To CELIE.*) What's this? Some sort of wickedness?
Black magic?

CELIE: No, sir! Strictly white.

MASCARILLE: (*To CELIE.*) I'll fill you in, if that's all right:
My master's smitten, barking mad
With love – he's got it *really* bad –
He wants a meeting, face to face,
With the young lady in the case
But that is proving rather hard
Thanks to a dragon who stands guard
Over this treasure day and night.
To worsen my poor master's plight
A rival's recently appeared –
Handsome – a rival to be *feared.*
Now, what my master needs to know
Is how, from here, it's going to go,
You have the answer, I've no doubt –
What are his chances?... Spit it out.

CELIE: Well... what star was he born beneath?

MASCARILLE: One that is constant, unto death –
As faithful as you could desire.

CELIE: About the *girl* I won't inquire.
As you were told, I know my stuff –
My science tells me quite enough:
She's spirited, and bold, and brave
Nobody's victim, no one's slave;
She *is* in love, though what she feels
She harbours sooner than reveals,
But – through my science – I can read
Her secret thoughts.

MASCARILLE: Can you indeed?
Amazing!

CELIE: Yes, and here they are:
If it's a constant one, his star,
And his intentions good, and pure,
The thing is virtually secure –
The fort that he's besieged *must* fall,
It wants to, and it will. That's all.

MARSCARILLE: The watchful *governor* of the fort
's an obstacle, I would have thought.

CELIE: A very tricky one, it's true –

79

MASCARILLE: The pesky...
CELIE: Here's what you must do...
(*Enter LELIE.*)
LELIE: There's no occasion for dismay
  This gentleman is my valet
  Don't worry, Monsieur Trufaldin:
  He only came to brooch my plan:
  Which is: to purchase and remove
  This lady here. If you approve
  And if the price suits both of us.
  The latter we should now discuss.
MASCARILLE: (*Aside.*) He's landed us right in the soup –
  Sweet Jesus, what a nincompoop!
TRUFALDIN: (*Aside.*) That's odd! their stories don't agree!
  Somebody's playing games with me.
MASCARILLE: (*To TRUFALDIN.*) Monsieur, this fellow's
                                       off his tree –
  A total loony – you know that.
TRUFALDIN: I do know this: I smell a rat.
  Célie, go in – at once.
  (*She obeys.*)
                            You two,
  You're shysters, rogues, the pair of you –
  When two men play a trick they fail
  Unless they tell a single tale –
  Try following that rule next time. (*He goes in.*)
MASCARILLE: Well, that was brilliant, quite sublime!
  The thing is going just as planned
  I have him eating from my hand
  Then *you* go sticking in your oar.
  What did you have to barge in for
  And contradict what I'd just said?
  And *you* call *me* a muttonhead!
LELIE: Just trying to help.
MASCARILLE: Of course you were!
  I don't know why I'm angry, sir,
  You've cocked up countless times before
  So what's one cock-up less or more?

Anything else would have been odd
Seeing you're such a silly sod.
LELIE: It isn't a complete *nightmare* –
I've done no harm we can't repair –
No need to chew me up for it.
What if our purchase plan *has* hit
A minor snag – that's not so bad.
But look: suppose *Léandre's* had
The same idea? Eh? Just suppose
He bids for her, cash on the nose?
That's something that we *must* prevent –
I'm right, no? Crisis management
Is what's required. I'll leave you be,
Last thing you want's more help from me,
But try and think of something – please.
MASCARILLE: In situations such as these
Money's what's wanted, but we've none.
We need a *ruse*. I'll think of one.
(*Exit LELIE, enter ANSELME.*)
ANSELME: What days we live in! *I* don't know!
It's such a ghastly farrago:
Absurd tight-fistedness, combined
With greed of the most naked kind –
Take lending money – it's the end:
People are in a rush to lend
But never, ever, to repay –
That is the way of things today –
Like having children – the first bit
Is fun – we plunge right into it
Without a qualm – then comes part two –
The accouchement of francs and sous
And what a struggle that can be!
Money will slip so easily
Into a purse, but you'll get nowt
When you attempt to prize it out –
So I should kneel now, and give thanks –
I've just got back two thousand francs.
MASCARILLE: How lucky he should come my way.
I'll pounce then, and secure my prey.

81

Buttering victims up works best
They have to be cajoled, caressed –
(*Aloud.*) Monsieur Anselme, you'll never guess...
(*Aside.*) Cajole cajole, caress caress...
(*Aloud.*) You'll never guess who I've just seen...
ANSELME: Pray tell.
MASCARILLE: That little minx Nerine.
ANSELME: Indeed? And did she mention me?
MASCARILLE: She did. She loves you – desperately.
ANSELME: She does?!
MASCARILLE: With all her main and might –
You've put her in a parlous plight.
ANSELME: What splendid news!
MASCARILLE: She's going to die.
'Anselme! Anselme!' you'll hear her cry.
'Anselme, my darling, when oh when,
Dearest and handsomest of men,
Will marriage come at last to douse
The fires of longing with its vows?'
ANSELME: But if her passion is that strong
Why's she concealed it for so long?
Young girls are a mysterious lot –
Am I... attractive, then, or what?
Even at my age, can I still...?
MASCARILLE: What? Cut the mustard? Fit the bill?
Pass sexual muster? Why, of course!
Look at that handsome face of yours –
Do I exaggerate? Perhaps.
You're not the *ugliest* of chaps
At any rate.
ANSELME: D'you really think...?
MASCARILLE: She's yours, monsieur. You're in the pink.
She's only got one end in view.
ANSELME: Really? What's that?
MASCARILLE: To marry you.
(*Under breath.*) Right here we go – let's snitch your purse.
(*He unbuttons the strap by which ANSELME's purse is
attached to his belt. It drops on the ground.*)

ANSELME: Pardon?
MASCARILLE: I said: she could do worse.
ANSELME: Splendid! You'd better prod her, though.
MASCARILLE: Prod her, sir? How d'you mean?
ANSELME: You know:
   Just cry me up, give me puff,
   Make her believe I'm cracking stuff.
MASCARILLE: Will do.
ANSELME: Good man! (*Going.*) Well – a bientot.
MASCARILLE: Ta ta.
   (*ANSELME is almost off the stage and MASCARILLE is*
   about to retrieve the purse.)
ANSELME: (*Coming back.*) Hang on a minute, though:
   I don't expect your help for free
   And you've already bolstered me
   By giving me this splendid news –
   No, anybody in my shoes
   Would offer you a quid pro quo –
   Some sort of small retainer...
   (*He is about to reach for his purse.*)
MASCARILLE: NO!!!
ANSELME: But I insist... (*Same business.*)
MASCARILLE: For God's sake, sir –
   I don't want tips – I'll speak to her
   Because I *want* you you to succeed –
ANSELME: Come come... (*Same.*)
MASCARILLE: No, really, there's no need!
   I'm acting out of pure good will.
ANSELME: That's really sweet of you, but still –
MASCARILLE: Sir, don't insult me.
ANSELME: Very well.
MASCARILLE: Stubborn old git!
   (*Again ANSELME goes, is almost off stage, and again*
   MASCARILLE is about to retrieve the purse when ANSELME
   comes back.)
ANSELME: Some bagatelle
   Or bauble – to encourage her –
   I would have thought was de rigueur –
   I'd like to send her one, through you

So choose one, if you're willing to,
And here's to pay for what you get...
(*Again he is about to reach for his purse.*)
MASCARILLE: No, wait! I don't need money yet –
I've *found* a bagatelle, you see,
And if she likes it, obviously
We'll have to pay – I'll let you know
How much it comes to.
ANSELME: Rightee-ho.
(*ANSELME is going, MASCARILLE is about to retrieve
the purse at last when ANSELME comes back again.*)
Give it her carefully. I mean
Make sure it leaves her no less keen.
(*ANSELME is going, stage left, when LELIE enters, stage
right, sees the purse, stage right, picks it up and comes forward
with it*)
LELIE: This purse was lying in the road.
ANSELME: (*Returning.*) I must have dropped it. Well I'm
                                          blowed!
Suppose you hadn't found it, eh?
And maybe later in the day
I'd noticed it had gone and thought
Some thief had pinched it. Lord! Distraught
I would have been – I'm in your debt –
I'll pay you back, but not just yet –
Call on me soon. (*Exit.*)
MASCARILLE: Bravo! Well played!
This seems to be your stock in trade –
The great last minute masterstroke.
LELIE: Good job I came, or he'd be broke.
MASCARILLE: Of course, monsieur. You're all we need.
Keep on like this and we'll succeed,
We cannot fail!
LELIE: Did I do wrong?
MASCARILLE: Was Atlas tall? Was Samson strong?
The fact is, you're an idiot.
I have to tell you, do I not?
I mean, I *am* entitled to?
Christ, here you are, without a sou,

And with a rival threatening you,
I'm just about to save the day
(Risking me my own neck, I may say.)
I'm pulling off a brilliant coup
When what does bird-brain go and do?
LELIE: You mean... the purse...?
MASCARILLE: He's fathomed it!
That was our source of funds, you twit!
LELIE: Oh, dear! But how was I to guess?
MASCARILLE: By thinking more and acting less?
LELIE: Next time you'd better warn me.
MASCARILLE: Fine,
I'll carry an enormous sign
Saying: I'M TRYING TO ROB THIS MAN.
Meanwhile, I have another plan,
A really wonderful idea
And this time *please* don't interfere.
LELIE: Of course I won't. I swear to you
That nothing will I say or do
To spoil the broth or rock the boat.
MASCARILLE: Just looking at you gets my goat –
Please go away.
LELIE: But do be quick
In case...
MASCARILLE: Just GO!
(*Exit LELIE.*)
                    It's a neat trick –
If all goes smoothly – well, let's see –
Here comes my man.
(*Enter PANDOLFE.*)
PANDOLFE: Oh, Mascarille!
MASCARILLE: Monsieur Pandolfe! What's up?
PANDOLFE: My son.
Please find me a replacement one.
This one is driving me insane.
LELIE: My master? *Isn't* he a *pain?*
The antichrist, the pits, the end –
He drives me round the blinking bend.

85

PANDOLFE: Thought you were thick as thieves, you two.
MASCARILLE: Monsieur, that simply isn't true.
    My goodness, if you only knew...
    I badger him for all I'm worth
    To *do his duty* and so forth
    I take him up on *everything*
    Perpetually arguing
    We are – we were just now, indeed
    (Not that he paid me any heed.)
    About that girl – the one you've said
    The little scoundrel is to wed,
    Old Anselme's daughter, *Hippolyte* –
    For insolence he's hard to beat –
    He simply won't do as he's told
    He's proud, and reckless, wild and bold –
    She's not for him. It makes me mad
    To think what toil and strife you've had
    Trying to bring the boy to heel –
    Respect is something he can't feel
    The boy's a lost case, I'm afraid.
PANDOLFE: You quarreled?
MASCARILLE: Quite a fuss I made.
PANDOLFE: Did you indeed? I'd always thought
    You were his rogue of first resort,
    The brains behind his crazy schemes.
MASCARILLE: Weeell, that's the way of things, it seems,
    Those who have earned it get no praise
    That's how the world wags nowadays.
    But, sir, if you could see the way
    I act, not just as his valet,
    But as his mentor, tutor, guide,
    How hard and ceaselessly I've tried
    To keep him on the Path of Good –
    You'd put my wages up, you would!
    'Master,' (I say.) 'for Heaven's sake!
    'You're causing us too much heart-ache
    With your mad antics – trim your sails –
    Ah! Woe betide the son who fails
    A father – I mean any one –

But *yours,* that *saint,* that *paragon!*
You have reduced him to despair
Can't you reform, or don't you care?
Just copy *him* – do *right* for once!
PANDOLFE: Splendid! And what was his response?
MASCARILLE: Response? He treats it like a joke,
　Talks tosh to put me off my stroke,
　Deep in his soul there lurks a seed
　(And I mean very deep indeed.)
　A seed of sense, or maybe two
　(Both he's inherited from you.)
　But these are seldom uppermost,
　His brain is buzzing with a host
　Of schemes, desires, in full career –
　If I could speak up, without fear,
　He'd knuckle under like a shot...
PANDOLFE: Then speak.
MASCARILLE:　　　　　I'd be in quite a spot
　If he found out that I'd let on
　But then, if you're a paragon
　It follows that you are discreet.
PANDOLFE: I like your reasoning, very neat.
　So: how exactly has he strayed?
MASCARILLE: By falling for a scullery-maid –
　Scullery-maid's a flattering word –
　The girl's a slave.
PANDOLFE:　　　　　Hmm. So I'd heard.
　I wanted confirmation, though,
　And you've supplied it.
MASCARILLE:　　　　　This should show
　Just where my loyalties really lie –
　I *have* done right, sir, haven't I?
PANDOLFE: Certainly. I must think how best
　To bring him round.
MASCARILLE:　　　　Might I suggest
　A method? Easy, quick, discreet?
　(I'm scared to speak, though – I'm dead meat
　If this gets back to him, monsieur.)
　The best way is: to *purchase* her

And get her well away. For this
Employ *Anselme,* and you can't miss –
Her owner, Trufaldin, and he
Are old associates, you see –
The whole thing can be done today –
He buys her for you, right away,
And then lets *me* take charge of her
So I can find a purchaser.
I have some contacts in the trade –
A decent offer should be made –
I get you back your whole outlay
At once, she's taken far away
And, with no slave-girl to compete,
Lélie comes round to Hippolyte.
But while that girl is living here
His love for her will interfere
With *any* match you make for him –
Even assuming he gives in
And marries who you tell him to
God knows what trouble will ensue.
PANDOLFE: How true! You're terribly astute.
I think I *shall* pursue this route.
I'll find Anselme, get the girl bought
(God damn her.) and then have her brought
Straight to you.
MASCARILLE: Good. I'll do the rest.
(*PANDOLFE goes.*)
That filled me with a sudden zest
For knavery, and knaves – hoorah!
What an amazing lot we are!
Ten minutes very shrewdly spent –
Must tell my master how it went.
(*He is about to go when enter HIPPOLYTE.*)
Ah! Hippolyte!
HIPPOLYTE: (*Beside herself.*) I overheard –
You treacherous swine, you! – every word!
I've caught you out! A good job, too –
I'd never have suspected you –
You're such a master of deceit!

MASCARILLE: Don't get excited, Hippolyte.
HIPPOLYTE: I love Léandre – you agreed
    To help me there – (*Sarcastic.*) such help I need!
    I trusted you to rescue me
    From this damned marriage to Lélie –
    You'd thwart my father's plans, you said –
    You're not, you're *furthering* them instead!
MASCARILLE: Hang on a minute! Slow down please!
    Why is your bonnet full of bees!
    You really should have stopped and thought
    Before you launched this wild onslaught
    Going at me nail and tooth –
    Oh well, you'd better know the truth.
HIPPOLYTE: The truth, indeed! You mean more lies!
    You've pulled the wool over my eyes
    For too long. What can you deny?
    I heard the whole thing, didn't I?
MASCARILLE: But it's to *him* that I've just *lied.*
    For Heaven's sake, I'm on your side!
    Look here: your father buys Célie,
    Hands her immediately to me,
    I hand her to my master – there!
    Both fathers caught in the same snare,
    Your father needs a son-in-law
    He's lost the one he'd opted for
    So he accepts Leandre instead –
    Bullseye – the whole thing's put to bed.
HIPPOLYTE: So that was all to help my cause?
MASCARILLE: That's right. But spare me your applause.
    You're on your own now, I'm afraid –
    If this is how my work's repaid
    I wash my hands of the affair.
    Your jibes are more than I can bear.
    So I'm a traitor and a swine,
    A master of deceit? Well, fine,
    You can sort out your own damned mess. (*Makes to go.*)
HIPPOLYTE: But I was in extreme distress –
    I'd no idea that you... Be fair!

MASCARILLE: Marry my master. I don't care.
My methods bother you, that's clear,
From now on I won't interfere,
I'll tell Pandolfe the plan went wrong
And you'll end up where you belong
In Monsieur Lelie's bed. Goodbye.
We clearly don't see eye to eye. (*Makes to go.*)
HIPPOLYTE: (*Holding on to him.*) Wait! Must you be so
drastic? Please!
Don't turn on someone when she sees
That she was wrong, and there's no need,
And when she's ready to concede
That she misjudged you. *Please* don't sulk –
One little tiff and off you skulk.
(*She has produced a purse.*)
Look – here – how much to make you stay?
MASCARILLE: I won't go. I'm not made that way.
I'd never leave you high and dry.
But to accuse me of a *lie,*
Impugn my *honour,* oh, *madame!*
You *know* what kind of man I am –
How *could* you?!
HIPPOLYTE: Mmm. A grave mistake.
What difference would two ducats make?
(*She holds them out. He pockets them.*)
MASCARILLE: It's fine. I may be sensitive,
I'm also ready to forgive,
One takes these insults, from a friend.
HIPPOLYTE: I long to know how this will end.
Will your plan work? Will he and I –
Oh, Mascarille.
MASCARILLE: We can but try.
Look, if the first plan does fall flat
I'll have more rabbits in my hat.
Relax, my dear. We cannot fail.
HIPPOLYTE: You'll profit, if we do prevail.
Leandre will show his gratitude.
MASCARILLE: D'you think my motives are so crude?
Money is something I pooh-pooh.

(Enter LELIE, looking as though he needs MASCARILLE.)
HIPPOLYTE: Your master wants a word with you.
    I'll leave you – do your best for me. (*Goes.*)
LELIE: Why are you dawdling, Mascarille?
    My plans would all have come unstuck
    But for a marvellous stroke of luck:
    I'd given up my dreams of bliss,
    Was staring into the abyss
    When who should I just chance to meet
    Leading my darling down the street?
    Anselme! He'd bought her! Made her his!
    Had *I* not intervened, that is,
    Parried the blow, foiled the attack
    Forced Trufaldin to take her back.
MASCARILLE: Ye gods! You know what you've *just done?*
    You've put us right back to square one.
    And for the third time! Stone the crows!
    You just enjoy it, I suppose –
    You *like* to exercise your knack
    For setting all my efforts back.
    You've got a genius for it.
    That was the whole plan, you half-wit!
    Anselme was going to hand her over
    To *me* – we would have been in clover.
    This is the last straw. I resign.
    I'd rather be your cow, your swine,
    And wind up as a steak or joint
    Than work for you. What *is* the point?
    No, since I neither grunt nor moo
    I'm off, I'm out, that's it, we're through,
    I've had it up to *here* with you! (*He storms off.*)
LELIE: A bit of booze and he'll be fine.
    Let's find a tavern and some wine. (*Goes off after him.*)

End of Act One.

ACT TWO

Scene 1

MASCARILLE: Alright, alright, monsieur, you win.
    I'm going to help you. I give in.
    If I resigned I now retract,
    Heaven knows why, I must be cracked.
    I can't say no – it's just as well
    I'm not a woman. Let me *spell*
    This message out though, once again,
    Just to be sure I've made it plain:
    If you stick in your stupid oar
    And undo all my work *once more*
    It *will* be curtains. *Is* that clear?
LELIE: I'll temporarily disappear.
MASCARILLE: No meddling whatsoever?
LELIE: None.
MASCARILLE: Alright, then, this is what I've done:
    I've killed your dad – that is, I've *said*
    To various people that he's dead –
    He's had an apoplectic fit.
    That was my tale. To bolster it
    I've made the old man disappear –
    I lied – I gave him the idea
    That, buried in a plot of ground
    On his estate, some gold's been found,
    Unearthed by builders working on
    His country house. So off he's gone
    To get a first sight of his gold,
    Accompanied by the whole household,
    Everyone else but us has gone,
    I've even drafted in someone
    To be his corpse. We'll bury him
    This afternoon. I've filled you in
    Now all I'm asking you to do
    Is help to make this lie seem true.
    It ought to go off like a dream. (*Goes.*)

LELIE: It's rather a macabre scheme!
  However, I'll do anything –
  The happiness success will bring,
  The blissful end, must justify
  Whatever means I choose to try,
  And certainly a harmless lie.
  (*MASCARILLE returns with ANSELME.*)
  He's back! With Anselme! That was quick! (*Goes.*)
ANSELME: I mean, he wasn't even sick!
  He might at least have got ill first.
  It all seems rather... unrehearsed.
MASCARILLE: It's irritating, I agree.
ANSELME: How badly has it hit Lelie?
MASCARILLE: Poor boy! He wishes *he* was dead –
  He beats his breast, his arms, his head,
  Most of his body's black and blue –
  It's obvious what I have to do:
  Bury the old man right away –
  Because the longer we delay
  The more the boy will contemplate
  The horror of his father's fate
  And maybe do some desperate act –
  I must move fast, today, in fact,
  To get the body underground.
ANSELME: That doesn't seem entirely sound.
  Quick burials suggest foul play.
MASCARILLE: I promise you, he slipped away
  As you or I'd have wanted to.
  But anyway, to continue,
  My master's keen to do things right
  To ease his pain (I think it might.)
  He means to bury the old man
  With *dignity*, or that's the plan –
  The trouble is, it's going to cost
  Because, in view of what he's lost,
  Some *style* is what we're looking for
  Some *pomp*. Of course, he won't be poor,
  Not when they've dealt with the estate
  But all the business of probate

And deeds and bonds to liquidate
Is going to mean a long delay
Before some money comes his way.
He's in a hurry, which is why
He thought of giving *you* a try –
He wondered if you'd lend a hand
A short term loan, you understand,
Until they sort out the estate.
ANSELME: Well, if it really cannot wait
I'll help him out. (*Goes.*)
MASCARILLE: We're almost there.
Just needs some cunning and some care. (*Goes.*)

Scene 2

Same, a little later.

ANSELME: To think, this morning, he was here
Alive and well – and now – oh, dear!
It feels so tragic and so strange.
MASCARILLE: Time does that, though. It brings on change.
It's there to damage and destroy.
LELIE: Ah!
ANSELME: Mascarille is right, my boy,
Face facts: your father was a man –
Could he escape death? No one can.
LELIE: Ah!
ANSELME: Yes, it's all Death ever does –
Plot how to do away with us.
LELIE: Ah!
ANSELME: We can pour out endless prayers –
D'you think he hears? D'you think he cares?
It doesn't sway him in the least
He's just a ravening, murderous beast.
LELIE: Ah!
MASCARILLE: (*To ANSEME.*) Oh, monsieur, you're
                                    talking sense
But, look, his grief is too intense
For words to sooth or salve.

ANSELME: Alright,
  Let there at least be some respite,
  Some moderation in his pain.
LELIE: Ah!
MASCARILLE: (*To ANSELME.*) Told you. All attempts are
                                                    vain.
ANSELME: Anyway, he can count on me.
  I'll fetch some cash immediately
  To pay for decent obsequies
  So he can properly appease
  His father's shade.
LELIE: Ah! Ah!
MASCARILLE: (*To ANSELME.*) Hear that?
  Saying that word's like throwing fat
  Onto a fire. He's *so* upset.
ANSELME: There's a small matter of some debt –
  I owed your father quite a sum
  As you'll discover when you come
  To sort out his estate. Therefore
  You're due a funeral, and more
  From me – but please be in no doubt,
  Lelie, that, with debts or without
  You could have counted on my aid.
LELIE: Ah!
ANSELME: One small detail, I'm afraid –
  I shall require a signed receipt.
MASCARILLE: That's a demand he just can't meet –
  Not in his present mental state.
LELIE: Ah!
MASCARILLE: Soon the tempest will abate –
  I'll organise one for you then.
  But now you've set *me* off again –
  I feel some fresh grief coming on –
  (*Pretends to burst into tears.*)
  Oh, God! I can't believe he's gone –
  For hours on end my heart has bled –
  I'm off – I've got more tears to shed.
  (*Exit MASCARILLE, dragging LELIE off with him.*)

95

ANSELME: Life's fluctuations are bizarre
 And, Lord, how vulnerable we are,
 Each one of us, to fortune's whim.
 (*Enter PANDOLFE.*)
 By God and all the Saints, it's him!
 Pandolfe! Then was he just asleep?
 (*To PANDOLFE.*) Get back! You're making my flesh creep!
 Get back, I say! God, he looks grim!
 Death's knocked the stuffing out of him!
 STAY BACK!
PANDOLFE: Anselme, old man, what's wrong?
ANSELME: Go back a yard – no, a furlong –
 Then tell me what has brought you here:
 Why have you chosen to appear?
 Perhaps you've come to say goodbye.
 It's awfully nice of you, but I
 Can do without such politesse
 It causes me too much distress
 If you're in torment and require
 Some prayers to save you from Hellfire
 Then you can count on me: I'll pray.
 I promise. Now, please go away,
 Your scaring me.
PANDOLFE: The man's insane!
 (*To ANSELME.*) You think I'm dead? Well, think again.
ANSELME: I *saw* your corpse, for Heaven's sake!
PANDOLFE: You did? Oh! Then it's *my* mistake!
 I still *feel* pretty lively, though.
ANSELME: You do seem... *blithe*... as corpses go.
 Your loss has come as quite a blow.
 When I was told – by Mascarille –
 It chilled my heart, it shattered me.
PANDOLFE: Are you awake or dreaming, man?
 It's *me, Pandolfe*, none other than!
ANSELME: Or else a fiend whose donned his shape
 As part of some infernal jape.
PANDOLFE: I could pretend that I *was* one,
 Lead you a dance, and have some fun,

But I've no time for games today –
Something's afoot, I smell foul play:
A tale of treasure trove, which I
Have just discovered was a lie,
And now your thinking I was dead –
These little oddities have bred
A dark suspicion in my brain:
What single thing can best explain
Such nonsense? Who's the world's worst rogue?
Who'd practice the whole catalogue
Of knavery, without remorse
Or scruple? Mascarille, of course.
ANSELME: Of course! It's all some sort of plot,
    I'm a complete and utter clot!
    I've let him make an ass of me!
    I'm counting on your secrecy –
    I'd be disgraced if this got out –
    Please help me – we must set about
    Recovering the gold I gave!
PANDOLFE: For what?
ANSELME: Your funeral, and grave.
PANDOLFE: So it's extortion? I'm afraid
    It's no use counting on *my* aid –
    I've other fish to fry – I hope
    To see him dangling from a rope.
ANSELME: Who? Mascarille?
PANDOLFE: Who else?
    (*Exit PANDOLFE.*)
ANSELME: A dupe,
    A credulous old nincumpoop,
    The stupidest of fools and nits –
    I've lost my money and my wits.
    I mean to say, you would have thought
    That I'd have checked out his report,
    Such tripe as that should not be taken
    On trust!
    (*Enter LELIE with a fat purse.*)
LELIE: This purse has saved my bacon!
    I'm off to buy my love. Hooray!

(*He turns a little, joyous pirouette.*)
ANSELME: (*Heavy sarcasm.*) Doing as I advised you, eh,
  Setting aside your grief? Bravo!
LELIE: Setting aside? I'll have you know,
  I'll *grieve* until my dying day.
ANSELME: I'll take that purse back, if I may –
  Some of the coins are counterfeit,
  But that's the trend now, isn't it?
  On every street-corner you meet
  Another evil, lying cheat,
  Hanging's too good for 'em, I say –
  I meant to throw the duds away
  But somehow stupidly forgot –
  I shall replace them, worry not.
LELIE: Counterfeit coins? I don't think so.
  Thank you for being careful, though.
ANSELME: I'm certain some of them are fake –
  Give me the purse, for safety's sake –
  False coins are never hard to spot.
  (*LELIE hands it over.*)
  Good. Excellent. Is this the lot?
LELIE: Yes.
ANSELME: Splendid! Oh, my darling gold,
  You're mine again to have and hold,
  Back in your proper place, my purse!
  (*To LELIE.*) And you, you rogue, you fiend, and worse,
  Are rightly penniless again:
  You go around, killing old men
  Who are in fact quite fit and well –
  The future son-in-law from Hell,
  That's what you are! What grisly fate
  Were you about to fabricate
  For *me,* the father of your bride,
  What foul, fictitious homicide?!
  My, but you've played a treacherous game!
  You ought to wither, wilt with shame,
  Curl up into a ball and die.
  (*Exit ANSELME.*)

LELIE: I caught it that time, didn't I?
  Well, this is most inopportune.
  What put him on to us so soon?
  (*Enter MASCARILLE, triumphant.*)
MASCARILLE: How crafty can a swindler *be!*
  He brought the money, didn't he?
  I'll take it from you, then – may I?
  I've got a serving girl to buy.
  Your rival won't be overjoyed.
LELIE: My hopes of bliss have been destroyed!
  I shake my powerless fist at Fate!
MASCARILLE: Hey! Why are you in such a state?
LELIE: Because the outlook's very grim:
  Anselme found out we'd cheated him,
  He's just reclaimed his wretched gold –
  Quite an ingenious lie he told –
  He claimed some coins were false and said
  He'd bring me proper ones instead.
MASCARILLE: You're joking, aren't you?
LELIE: No. It's true.
MASCARILLE: Not really?
LELIE: Would I lie to you?
  Now I suppose you'll throw a fit.
MASCARILLE: And strain my heart? Don't count on it.
  Why would I risk my health for *you?*
  You'll have to rope in someone new
  Coz I can't help you any more –
  I'm sorry, this is the last straw,
  We're through.
LELIE: You know you don't mean that.
  For pity's sake, don't be a rat
  And scuttle off the sinking ship
  Because I made a tiny slip.
  Alright, so things have gone awry
  But I did good work, didn't I?
  My acting – brilliant, wasn't it?
  I had him fooled, you must admit,
MASCARILLE: You did all right.

LELIE: Damn right I did!
Not that I'm crowing. God forbid.
I'm well aware that I'm to blame
For this débacle. All the same,
If ever you did care for me
Please, sort out the catastrophe,
Help me, I beg you.
MASCARILLE: No. Goodbye.
LELIE: *Please,* Mascarille.
MASCARILLE: No. Why should I?
LELIE: I'll kill myself...
MASCARILLE: Fine. Go ahead.
LELIE: Won't you be sad to see me dead?
MASCARILLE: Not in the least.
LELIE: Look – here's the blade...
I'll stick it in... you won't be swayed...?
MASCARILLE: No. Stick away.
LELIE: Goodbye!
MASCARILLE: Tara.
LELIE: But...
MASCARILLE: What a ditherer you are!
Get on with it!
LELIE: You'd let me die!
I bet you've got your beady eye
On things of mine, my clothes maybe...
MASCARILLE: It's no use trying to blackmail me –
You haven't stuck the blade in yet –
It's obviously an empty threat.
(*TRUFALDIN comes out of his house with LEANDRE.*)
LELIE: Léandre! With Trufaldin! Oh, no!
He's going to buy her!
MASCARILLE: I hope so.
And serve you right – I said before
Not to go sticking in your *oar.*
LELIE: Oh, God! What *am* I going to do?
MASCARILLE: I haven't got the foggiest clue.
LELIE: I'll quiz him and create a spat.
MASCARILLE: And what would be the point of that?

LELIE: I must do something, mustn't I?
If *you* won't help...
MASCARILLE: Alright, I'll try.
It's just not in me to be mean –
I shall discreetly try and glean
What the boy's up to.
TRUFALDIN: (*To LEANDRE.*) Splendid! Done.
(*They shake hands and TRUFALDIN goes back into his house.*)
MASCARILLE: I'll make him trust me, that's step one,
Then find out what he plans to do,
Then somehow not allow him to.
LEANDRE: Now I am happy. After this
Surely the fortress of my bliss
Must be impossible to breach
She is beyond my rival's reach.
MASCARILLE: Help! Help me, someone! Anyone!
He's killing me!
LEANDRE: What's going on?
MASCARILLE: I'm black and blue from all his blows!
LEANDRE: Did Lélie beat you? Why?
MASCARILLE: God knows!
He's flayed the hide right off me, though.
And I'm dismissed.
LEANDRE: You poor fellow!
Where does it hurt?
MASCARILLE: Here, here, and there,
My back, my shoulders, everywhere!
(*Addressing where LELIE has just exited.*)
You'll pay for this! A serving man,
That's all I've ever been or am,
I'm meant to be at your command
But I'm not dirt, d'you understand?
Four years of sweat and toil, repaid
With what? A broken shoulder blade!
You've gone too far! You're going to pay!
I'll be avenged on you, I say!
That bit of stuff that's caught your eye
That slave girl you're so smitten by

That *I* was to going to get for you?
Well, I'm not damn well going to!
I'll work for someone else instead
And see she ends up in *his* bed!
LEANDRE: Relax! Don't get so overwrought!
Look, Mascarille, I've always thought
Most highly of you, as you know –
You are a gem, as servants go,
Diligent, loyal, pure gold all round –
Cheer up! I think you may have found
Another master.
MASCARILLE: Thank you, sir!
You want that girl? I'll get you her.
What better way of paying back
That servant-thrashing maniac?
I've got a plan, it's watertight –
You'll have your Célie by tonight.
LEANDRE: Don't bother – she's already mine.
Strange that a creature so divine
Should have a price! She had one, though –
How could I let the bargain go?
I snapped her up.
MASCARILLE: You did? I see!
LEANDRE: In fact, if only I were free
I'd show her to you. As things stand
I'm not exactly in command
Of my own fate – my father is
And it's a latest whim of his
(A letter has just told me this.)
That I should marry Hippolyte.
I don't imagine he would greet
My present enterprise with glee,
It calls for total secrecy:
I've told her owner that I have
A friend, who wants to buy the slave,
For whom I'm acting. He's been paid.
Someone will call on him, I've said,
Who'll show this ring of mine to prove

His bona fides, and remove
Célie, or that's what we've agreed.
But after that I'm going to need
A place where she can safely hide.
MASCARILLE: I know a place, sir, just outside
The city that should meet the case –
An old aunt's house which I can place
At your disposal. Trust in me –
I absolutely guarantee
That nobody on earth will know.
LEANDRE: You *are* the man, then! I thought so!
Here, take my ring, collect Célie,
Only be sure to let him see
This crucial token in your hand –
Then take her to your aunt's house, and...
(*Sees HIPPOLYTE approaching.*) Uh-oh!
(*Enter HIPPOLYTE.*)
HIPPOLYTE: Leandre, I have news,
Tidings of joy perhaps, but whose?
Mine, possibly – but yours? who knows?
LEANDRE: I'd better hear it, I suppose.
HIPPOLYTE: (*Holding out her hand to him.*) Come, then –
I'll tell you on the way.
LEANDRE: Where to?
HIPPOLYTE: The temple.
LEANDRE: (*Whispers to MASCARILLE.*) Don't delay!
Go! NOW! And serve me faithfully.
(*Exeunt HIPPOLYTE and LEANDRE.*)
MASCARILLE: I'll serve you – à la Mascarille.
My master's such a lucky boy!
When he hears this he'll die of joy!
First to have lost the girl and then
To steal her from the lion's den –
The man he thought had taken her!
Well, this is going to cause a stir!
A hero – that's what this makes me,
A *master* of skullduggery.
TRUFALDIN: (*Above.*) Who's there?

MASCARILLE: This *ring's* my calling card.
(*He shows the ring.*)
TRUFALDIN: I'll get her. Wait out in the yard.
(*TRUFALDIN goes into the house. Enter MESSENGER.*)
MESSENGER: Good day, sir. If you wouldn't mind –
I need to know where I can find
One Trufaldin.
(*TRUFALDIN comes out of the house with CELIE.*)
TRUFALDIN: Sir, I am he.
Well? What is it you want with me?
MESSENGER: Nothing, I'm just a messenger –
(*Hands him the letter.*) I think it might be urgent, sir..
TRUFALDIN: (*Reads.*) Madrid, March twentieth: – Dear
sir: Heaven, Providence, my guiding star, call it what
you will, has intervened on my behalf. I have just
learned, and what joyful news it is, that my daughter,
who was kidnapped by brigands four years ago, is now
your slave, having assumed the alias of Célie. If ever
you have known what it is to be a father, if ever you
have felt the tender ties of kinship, I beseech you, guard
my beloved daughter for me as if she were your own.
I am on my way now to collect her, and I will reward
you generously for your pains – so generously that you
will forever after bless the day when it fell within your
power to assist me. I remain, sir, your most obedient
servant, Don Pedro de Gusman, Marquess of Montalcane.
Spaniards are such a devious lot
I might dismiss all this as rot.
However, when I bought Célie
The vendor did let on to me
That somebody might soon appear
To claim her; and he made it clear
That if they did, they'd pay top rate –
But there I was, I wouldn't wait,
I almost let the best deal slip –
A minute later and your trip
Would have been wasted – this man here
Had come for her. But have no fear,
(*Tapping the letter.*) I *shall* comply with this request.

(*To MASCARILLE.*) Monsieur, I think it might be best
If we forgot this after all,
Please tell your client he's to call
And get his money back.
MASCARILLE: What cheek!
You can't just change your...
TRUFALDIN: Please don't speak,
Just go.
(*TRUFALDIN goes back into his house, MASCARILLE and
the MESSENGER go their separate ways.*)
MASCARILLE: We're in the soup again
Thanks to this thunderbolt from Spain –
One minute riding high, the next
Knocked down – I'm thoroughly perplexed.
(*Enter LELIE, laughing to himself.*)
MASCARILLE: You seem extremely blithe and gay –
Why, might I ask?
LELIE: Before I say
Just let me laugh a little more.
MASCARILLE: Do, till you dislocate your jaw –
I'll join you – (*Heavy sarcasm.*) things have gone *so* well.
(*MASCARILLE laughs, a sour, sardonic laugh.*)
LELIE: You're never going to give me Hell
Again, you know, or rant and roar
At me for 'sticking in my oar'.
It's true, at times I am *headstrong* –
I go too fast and get things wrong,
But I *am* clever, and possess
Imagination nonetheless –
You won't be quite so quick to scoff
When you hear what I've just pulled off.
MASCARILLE: Impress me, if you think you can.
LELIE: Seeing Léandre with Trufaldin
Completely put the wind up me –
To ward off a catastrophe
Was now my all-consuming aim
And from my ruminations came
A trick so neat, and deftly played
That it puts all yours in the shade.

MASCARILLE: You wrote to Trufaldin.
LELIE: I did!
    Pretending I was in Madrid –
    Assuming the identity
    Of a great nobleman.
MASCARILLE: I see.
LELIE: I told him...
MASCARILLE: Don't go on. I know.
LELIE: You haven't heard the best bit, though.
    My letter reached him just in time:
    But for this masterstroke of mine
    (I heard this from my messenger.)
    Somebody would have taken her –
    He all but had her in his grip
    (And how's this for oneupmanship?)
    When my amazing missive came –
    By half an inch he missed his aim –
    You must admit, a brilliant coup –
    But did I hear you say you knew?
MASCARILLE: I think I'd better leave you.
LELIE: Why?
    I did superbly, didn't I?
    So, do I get some praise or what?
MASCARILLE: What praise is that? For being a clot,
    A bungling dolt, a mindless goon,
    A meddling, featherbrained buffoon
    Whose knack for making things fall through
    Language cannot do justice to?
    I'm going. Please don't follow me.
LELIE: I must, to solve this mystery.
MASCARILLE: All right then, how fast can you run?
    (*Runs off.*)
LELIE: What does he mean? What have I done?
    And why is he avoiding me?
    Oh, heck! I'm totally at sea!
    (*He dashes off after MASCARILLE.*)

End of Act Two.

ACT THREE

MASCARILLE: I can't be kind to him again.
Forgiving him would be insane.
Trick after trick I try to play
And each time *he* gets in the way,
Why can't he let me do my stuff?
Well that was it, I've had enough.
Just one thing makes me hesitate –
I'm justifiably irate
But if I throw the towel in now
I'll never get to take my bow –
People'd simply think I'd failed
And couldn't get the problem nailed.
I'm famed for being smart and sly –
I'd have to kiss that fame goodbye...
All right, I'll give it one last try –
To keep my place on history's page
I'll swallow back my righteous rage.
But what to do? No scheme's immune
To scuppering by that brainless loon!
Whatever I devise he'll spoil
I produce order from turmoil
He creates chaos out of that
He's got the process right off pat.
Ah, well, once more into the breach –
This plan had better be a peach
And if he ballses up *once* more
There's *no more help,* I'm out the door,
We go our separate ways right there,
This is my *last attempt,* I *swear!*
(*Thinks.*) The whole procedure ought to prove
Much easier if I can remove
Léandre, our rival, from the scene –
A bramble in our path he's been...
Now, just suppose the boy should tire
Of his pursuit, if his desire
Should flag, and he give up the chase...

That's one less pest around the place,
In fact, by far the biggest one –
The rest is very simply done... (*Thinking hard.*)
I have it now, my master-plan!
And here he comes, the very man.
(*Enter LEANDRE.*)
Sir, I'm afraid it was no go.
He went back on his word.
LEANDRE: I know.
The girl belongs to some grandee
Some Spanish marquess, doesn't she?
He's going to claim her... what hogwash!
Lelie invented all that tosh
To try and stop me buying her.
So I've just learned.
MASCARILLE: The lying cur!
LEANDRE: But Trufaldin has swallowed it.
He won't believe it's all bullshit.
MASCARILLE: You'd better give her up.
LEANDRE: What for?
Give up the woman I adore?
By hook or crook she *will* be free
And *I* shall have her. If need be
I'll marry her!
MASCARILLE: You won't?!
LEANDRE: I will.
Her origins *are* doubtful. Still,
She has attractions which outweigh
That obstacle.
MASCARILLE: And what are they?
LEANDRE: Oh – beauty, virtue, charm.
MASCARILLE: *Virtue?*
Hmmm...
LEANDRE: 'Hmmm' means what?
MASCARILLE: I can't tell you.
No, if I did you'd get upset.
You look narked now.
LEANDRE: I'm not – not yet.
Just spit it out, please.

MASCARILLE: Oh, all right,
Perhaps it's time you saw the light –
She can't... she's not... she likes...
LELIE: Go on.
MASCARILLE: Look, sir, she'll sleep with anyone.
I would say: at the drop of a hat
Except she's even worse than that,
The hat does not have time to drop –
Given the chance, she'd never stop –
She *seems* chaste, but it's all an act.
The girl's a slut and that's a fact,
This is one thing I know about,
I can just *sniff* loose women out.
LEANDRE: You think...?
MASCARILLE: Her virtue's a charade.
LEANDRE: No!
MASCARILLE: A chimera, a facade
That crumbles at the merest sight
Of *money*.
LEANDRE: NO, that *can't* be right...
MASCARILLE: Not that I'm stopping you. Feel free.
For God's sake, don't be ruled by me.
Marry the trollop, go ahead –
You'll have a crowded marriage bed!
LEANDRE: I can't... I don't believe my ears...
MASCARILLE: (*Aside.*) I've got him.
LEANDRE: A whole sea of tears
Could never wash away my grief!
I'm finished, shattered. (*He is starting to cry.*)
MASCARILLE: Handkerchief?
(*He proffers a handkerchief. LEANDRE takes it and blows
his nose.*)
LEANDRE: Go to the post office and see
If there's a package there for me.
(*Exit MASCARILLE.*)
Would anybody have believed...?
No face, or air, can have deceived
As utterly as Célie's do –
Assuming what he says is true.

(*Enter LELIE.*)
LELIE: What's up, Léandre? You look downcast.
  Why's your flag flying at half mast?
  What's caused this access of despair?
LEANDRE: Nothing, so far as I'm aware.
LELIE: You're not upset about Célie?
LEANDRE: As if I'd let *her* trouble *me!*
LELIE: You wanted her, but in the end
  You lost her, so you now pretend
  You never had her in your sights.
LEANDRE: Your little stratagems and sleights
  Are plain for anyone to read –
  If I was after Célie, we'd
  Soon see who had the smarter brain,
  You little shyster!
LELIE: Come again?
  What 'sleights' are you referring to?
LEANDRE: It's no use, mate, I'm on to you –
LELIE: I'm sorry? 'On to'? On to *what?*
LEANDRE: You, and your feeble little plot.
LELIE: Léandre, you're not making sense.
LEANDRE: By all means keep up this pretence,
  Meanwhile, I might make one thing clear:
  SHE DOESN'T INTEREST ME – d'you hear?
  She's shop-soiled, damaged, sorry stuff,
  A barge-pole isn't long enough
  To touch her with, but enough said,
  You put the trollop in your bed
  I won't be standing in your way.
  (You'll only be her tenth today.)
LELIE: Look here...!
LEANDRE: I've shocked him now! This *whore*
  Is yours, I tell you. I withdraw.
  I'm off. You take her, if you wish,
  She's certainly a tasty dish:
  So half the world has had a bit?
  I'm sure it's still worth tasting it!
LELIE: (*His hand is on his sword-hilt.*) I *will* not *hear* such
                                 things of *her!*

Listen, Léandre, I much prefer
A rival to a poisonous snake
Who slanders her for slander's sake.
LEANDRE: It isn't slander, though, it's true.
The girl's a jade, a whore.
LELIE: Says who?
LEANDRE: Someone on whom I can rely.
LELIE: The man's a scoundrel, and here's why:
There *are* no blemishes on *her* –
I would have seen them if there were –
I know her. She's an angel.
LEANDRE: No,
A *trollop* – *Mascarille* said so.
What's more, he knew whereof he spoke.
LELIE: Célie a trollop? What a joke!
He's lying.
LEANDRE: Why would he do that?
LELIE: If she's a whore I'll eat my hat.
You should have thrashed him black and blue
I would have murdered him!
LEANDRE: Me too –
Why would one let the fellow live?
Unless he had proof positive
That what he had alleged was true.
(*Enter MASCARILLE.*)
LELIE: Here comes the little swine. Hey, you!
(*Enter MASCARILLE.*)
MASCARILLE: Pardon?
LELIE: Come here! Yes, you, you *rat!*
(*MASCARILLE comes up.*)
What do you think you're playing at?
What business had you to malign
Someone so perfect, so *divine?*
Blacken *my* name, but not Célie's.
MASCARILLE: (*In a whisper.*) Sir, keep you trap shut this
                                                        time, *please* –
The whole point is: to make him think...
LELIE: You needn't whisper, nudge and wink,
I'm deaf, insensible and blind:

The girl I love has been maligned
Were it my brother, he would pay –
Just tell me what you've dared to say –
And if you wink at me once more…
MASCARILLE: What am I bothering with you for?
I'm off.
(*He's going. LELIE grabs him and pulls him back.*)
MASCARILLE: That hurt!
LELIE: *What have you said?*
MASCARILLE: (*Whispering again.*) Look, get this into your
                              thick head:
It's just a trick, a ruse, all right?
LELIE: Célie, a lady of the night?
(*Hitting him on each word.*)
A slut? A harlot? Take – it – BACK!
LEANDRE: Cut the poor man a *little* slack –
No need to hit him!
MASCARILLE: I give in:
Sir, if stupidity's a sin
Then *you* are going straight to Hell!
LELIE: (*To LEANDRE.*) I've got some choler to expel –
He *is* my servant, is he not?
I have a right to thrash him.
LEANDRE: What?!
Your servant? Still? (*To LELIE.*) I thought you said…
MASCARILLE: (*Aside.*) That's it. He's done it now. We're
                              dead.
LELIE: Yes. He's my servant. Mine to strike,
To kill, to anything-I-like.
LEANDRE: He works for *me* now.
LELIE: Works for *you?!*
Ha! Are you *totally* cuckoo?
MASCARILLE: (*Whispering again, and winking, and jerking
his head.*) Don't spoil it this time – *pleeeease*…
LELIE: Spoil what?
MASCARILLE: (*Aside.*) That's six debacles on the trot,
This fellow really *is* THE END –
Not *one* thing does he comprehend –
No word, no sign, no nothing. BLAST!

LELIE: (*To LEANDRE.*) Yes, he's my servant.
LEANDRE: Something passed
  Between you, didn't it? Today?
  You did dismiss him?
LELIE: Me? No way.
LEANDRE: Ah, but you thrashed him.
LELIE: I did *not!*
LEANDRE: Then it's all nonsense?
LELIE: Utter rot.
MASCARILLE: (*To LEANDRE.*) Sir, he's forgotten...
LEANDRE: It's no use:
  I smell a rat, another ruse.
  But I forgive you, Mascarille:
  Your master's disabusing me
  Makes up for your outrageous lies –
  You tried to trick me, I got wise –
  (*To LELIE.*) Our rivalry has just begun –
  You'll rue the day before I'm done –
  This is the start of the first act –
  Page one – the frontispiece, in fact! (*Goes.*)
MASCARILLE: (*Heavy sarcasm.*) We're in the pink. Hip-hip-
                              hoorah!
  It's all gone brilliantly so far!
LELIE: He said you'd said...
MASCARILLE: That's right. I lied.
  What's more, I'd almost rectified
  The situation: he'd bowed out.
  The rival army'd turned about
  And it was going to march away
  But could you let us win the day?
  Enjoy your triumph? Could you heck!
  If there's a plan for you to wreck
  You'll wreck it, and not turn a hair –
  No twerp in history can compare –
  You've got your twerping to a T!
LELIE: Couldn't you have alerted me?
  I'm bound to bungle everything
  If I don't know what's happening!

MOLIERE

MASCARILLE: Now, as a *sapper* you'd be fine –
The *speed* with which you undermine,
Explode each project I devise.
LELIE: What's done is done. It *would* be wise
To try and think up something new –
For that, of course, I count on you.
MASCARILLE: We've fallen out, though, haven't we,
So as to that, we'll have to see:
You've put me into quite a rage
It won't be easy to assuage –
But do me a good turn (or three)
And p'raps I *will* still help – We'll see.
LELIE: What do you want? My life? A limb?
I'd give one gladly.
MASCARILLE: Hark at him!
I know your type: you'd sooner fight
Than fork out half a franc.
LELIE: Oh, right!
So what you want is *money?*
MASCARILLE: No.
You *can* help with your father, though.
He's in a foul mood, really grim –
You must start pacifying him.
LELIE: I've *made* my peace with him.
MASCARILLE: That's great.
However, he's still in a bate
With *me.* I killed him, after all.
It's on *my* head the axe will fall.
· He's pressing charges, so I'm told.
You see, sir, with the frail and old
That's not the kind of lie you tell –
It's doesn't go down very well –
It gives them a *presentiment,*
Thoughts, which they naturally resent,
Of sickbeds, and the grave, and such.
I doubt if jail'd suit me much
And that is where he'll have me thrown.
He's really furious. You alone

Can still dissuade him from this course.
Don't put the cart before the horse:
Help *me,* and *then* I *might* help you.
Go and dissuade him. (*Motions him to get a move on.*)
LEANDRE: I'll try to. (*Going.*)
(*Coming back.*) But can't you think up some new
                         scheme...?
MASCARILLE: *We'll see!* Now GO, please!
(*Exit LELIE.*)
                         It would *seem*
That Trufaldin believes his lie
In which case, he won't kiss goodbye
To Célie yet – Léandre's stuck,
Time should be on our side, with luck,
For now, I think I'll call a halt
And not go rubbing yet more salt
Into the wound by thinking up a
Scheme that he'd only go and scupper.
I reckon...
(*Enter ERGASTE.*)
ERGASTE: Mascarille! Hello!
MASCARILLE: Ergaste?
ERGASTE: There's something you should know.
MASCARILLE: What's that?
ERGASTE: You're not to breathe a word.
(*Is about to tell him, then breaks off.*)
I hope we can't be overheard...
MASCARILLE: No, no.
ERGASTE: *Weeell...* it's about Célie –
Your master loves her, doesn't he?
Léandre, or so my sources say,
Is going to spirit her away
Having crept in there, in a mask,
'How will that work?' I hear you ask –
Well, the whole basis of his plan
Is that, most evenings, Trufaldin
Is visited by maskers.
MASCARILLE: Yes?

ERGASTE: Girls of the town in fancy dress.
Léandre will be exploiting this
To smuggle in some men of his.
MASCARILLE: Oh? Well, he hasn't got her yet.
I'll have to think what trap to set
To cheat him out of her... (*Thinks.*) Ah, yes –
That's nice – a bit of real finesse –
Mmmm, absolutely devilish –
I'll roast the boy in his own dish.
Thanks. Drinks on me when next we meet.
Tata.
(*Exit ERGASTE.*)
      Léandre's plan sounds neat –
If I could just *adapt* it now –
Get it to serve our turn somehow –
Avoid the risks involved in it
But still extract the benefit:
I'll beat him to it – *I* shall wear
A mask and sneak *myself* in there,
Get Célie out. Then in *he* goes –
Wearing a mask as well – who knows?
Suspicion could still fall on him,
In fact, I'll go out on a limb
And say it will – I mean to say
Word of his plan has found its way
To me already – how long, then,
Before nine people out of ten
Are talking of it? It's first rate –
He'll hand her to us on a plate.
Right then, to work – I've three main tasks:
Get help, some costumes, and some masks. (*Goes.*)
(*Enter LELIE and ERGASTE.*)
LELIE: Abductions?! Masquerades?!
ERGASTE: Just so.
One of his servants let me know
And I at once relayed the news
To Mascarille. He's got some ruse
To thwart Léandre, or so he said –

Devised it off the top of his head
He did, but since we've met like this –
Well, you'd have taken it amiss
If I'd not told you, wouldn't you?
LELIE: I'm grateful. And you will be too –
I'm going to make it worth your while.
My man will pull this off in style,
But not, perhaps, without *my* aid –
I won't, repeat won't, have it said
That I looked on, the lazy lout,
While *my* affairs were sorted out.
I have a pistol and a sword –
I'll leave Léandre dead or gored.
(*Exit ERGASTE. LELIE goes up to TRUFALDIN's house and calls.*)
Hello!
TRUFALDIN: (*Appearing at the window.*) Who's there?
LELIE: Sir, lock your door
With all the bolts tonight.
TRUFALDIN: What for?
LELIE: Some masked men will be coming here
To steal Célie from you.
TRUFALDIN: Oh, dear!
LELIE: They're dressed as girls. They're on their way.
But I'm here, ready for the fray. (*Rattling his sword.*)
(*He sees MASCARILLE and his MEN, masked and dressed as girls, approaching.*)
TRUFALDIN: Masked kidnappers! Heavens above!
LELIE: (*Challenging MASCARILLE.*) Where are you heading
                                        for, 'my love'?
(*Ogling 'her'.*) A good wine, judging by the cask –
Mind if I just remove this mask?
(*MASCARILLE is muttering something.*)
Why are you mumbling? May I?
(*LELIE tries to remove the mask, MASCARILLE eludes his efforts. TRUFALDIN comes out holding an enormous blunderbuss, which he points at MASCARILLE and his henchmen. The henchmen scatter. MASCARILLE remains.*)

TRUFALDIN: I'll bid you bunch of rogues goodbye.
(*To MASCARILLE.*) Be off with you, you thieving cur!
(*To LELIE.*) I'm very grateful to you, sir.
Goodnight.
(*TRUFALDIN disappears, the window shuts. MASCARILLE
removes his mask. LELIE takes it in, stunned by the discovery
of who it is.*)
LELIE: *Another* damned mistake?
Say it's not you, for pity's sake!
MASCARILLE: It isn't me. It's someone else.
LELIE: I've wrecked things yet again. Hell's bells!
How many more catastrophes?
You should have warned me!
MASCARILLE: Shut it, please.
That's it, goodbye, farewell, adieu,
This time I wash my hands of you!
LELIE: Where shall I turn?
MASCARILLE: Turn where you like.
As of this moment, *I'm* on strike.
LELIE: (*Kneels.*) Look, Mascarille, I'm on my knees –
Forgive my bungling *once* more... *pleeeease!*
I swear to God I never meant...
(*Enter LEANDRE and his men, also masked and dressed as girls.*)
MASCARILLE: (*Seeing them.*) Stop *whining* sir!
                              It's time we went.
(*They go.*)
LEANDRE: (*To MEN, very loudly.*) Sssh! Not a sound now, lads.
(*TRUFALDIN appears at the window again.*)
TRUFALDIN: Not *more!*
Will there be maskers at my door
All blinking night? Please, gentlemen,
If it's Célie you're after, then
I have to tell you, she's in bed,
No kidnappers tonight, she said,
She needs her sleep. Goodnight, my friends.
To thank you for your pains she sends
This gift.

(*He empties a pot of something foul over them, then disappears.*
The window shuts.)
LEANDRE: That doesn't smell too sweet!
(*To MEN.*) Let's beat a tactical retreat.
(*They go.*)

End of Act Three.

ACT FOUR

MASCARILLE: So: done for yet again, you dope.
LELIE: (*Aside.*) He's talking to me! There's still hope!
MASCARILLE: (*Aside.*) I'm softening. I know it's wrong
    But I just can't be riled for long.
    There's too much kind blood in my veins.
LELIE: I *will* reward you for your pains...
    If any money comes my way.
MASCARILLE: Since when did kindness ever pay?
    Now: first of all I'll fill you in
    So you can't say you haven been
    When yet again things go awry.
    I've fed old Trufaldin a lie –
    I came to him, with a great show
    Of kind concern, to let him know
    That fresh attempts to steal Célie
    Were being made, and he should be
    Extremely vigilant indeed.
    I told him he should pay no heed
    To certain tales about her birth –
    This morning's letter wasn't worth
    The paper it was written on.
    Proceeding, after that, to don
    A cloak of moral righteousness
    I spoke about the great distress
    I felt at this world's wicked ways
    And how I wished to end my days
    Employed by someone good, and just,
    To whom I wanted to entrust
    My patrimony (a small sum)
    And savings. When my time should come
    This master was to be my heir.
LELIE: Get to the point.
MASCARILLE: I'm getting there.
    The talk of money worked a treat.
    From then on he was easy meat,

I had him on a lead. What's more
That opening we've been looking for
To get you and the girl alone?
I think he's just provided one.
He told me how his long lost son
Had visited him in a dream.
That's what's inspired my latest scheme.
Seems he originally came
From Naples, where he bore the name
Of Giorgio Ruberti. Well,
One day the government almost fell,
The State suspected Giorgio
Of a seditious plot, and so
He was obliged to slip away
At dead of night, one fateful...
LELIE: Hey,
I hope there's not much more of this –
Couldn't we give the rest a miss?
MASCARILLE: You said you wanted to be told.
Can't you just let the tale unfold?
LELIE: It's vital?
MASCARILLE: Very, I'm afraid.
His wife and baby daughter stayed
In Naples, but they both soon died
As Giorgio was mortified
To learn. Heart-broken and bereft,
His son was all he now had left
(Besides his money). This same son,
A rather academic one,
Was called Horace and had been sent
For learning and for betterment
Off to Boulogne, with one Albert
Who was to supervise him there.
Giorgio wrote to them – he planned
To get them both back with him, and
To find a nice town where all three
Could live – but it was not to be –
Years passed, and neither hide nor hair
Of either Horace or Albert

Did Giorgio see. The rendez-vous
He gave them, and kept strictly to,
Was never kept by *them*. He came
To this town, where he took the name
Of Trufaldin.
LELIE: That *must* be it.
MASCARILLE: No. Here's the most important bit:
I've found a part for you to play:
I shall require you to portray
A young Armenian merchant who,
In *Turkey* lately, *saw* these two
LELIE: Horace and – what was it...?
MASCARILLE: Albert
You are to say you saw the pair
Alive and well. Why choose this route?
There are convincing aspects to it:
People quite often disappear,
Nabbed by some foreign buccaneer,
They're given up for dead, and then
Years later, they pop up again,
A meeting's fixed and they're returned
To the poor family concerned.
So you're to say you've had a sight
Of them, they've told you of their plight
And you've obligingly supplied
The means to buy their freedom. Phew!
That's quite a spiel I've given you!
What else? Ah yes: you couldn't wait
For them, it would have made you late
For business meetings – you've returned
With greetings from Horace, who's learned
About his father's moving here
And change of name, and who'll appear
Next week, but could you stay with him,
Trufaldin, in the interim?
I hope to God you've got all that.
LELIE: I can produce it all, off pat.
MASCARILLE: You're sure?

LELIE: Of course I'm sure. Trust me.
I've got a brilliant memory.
MASCARILLE: I'll just go over it again.
LELIE: It's lodged already in my brain.
MASCARILLE: All right, then, I'll set things in train.
LELIE: I've had a thought.
MASCARILLE: Good Lord!
LELIE: Horace –
I mean, I've never seen his face –
I can't describe him, if I'm asked?
MASCARILLE: When d'you suppose he saw him last,
You cretin? Years and years ago.
So will it be a problem? No.
Captivity, in any case,
Is bound to change a fellow's face,
LELIE: Suppose he recognises me?
MASCARILLE: He didn't take you in, did he?
He barely got a glimpse of you.
And your hat hid your face.
LELIE: That's true...
(*Thinks.*) What *town* in Turkey was this at?
MASCARILLE: My goodness, can't *you* think of that?
Try Tunis.
LELIE: Right. Away we go.
MASCARILLE: For God's sake, do be careful, though:
Don't attempt anything too smart –
Just keep it simple, play your part.
LELIE: Try and be smart? I'd rather die!
You wait: I'm going to act and lie
So smoothly he won't see the join.
MASCARILLE: (*Recapping.*) Horace a student in Boulogne
Albert his tutor, Trufaldin
A Neapol...
LELIE: For God's sake, man,
D'you think my head is made of wood?
MASCARILLE: Yes, more or less. (*Goes.*)
LELIE: That man's so good,
Respectful, till I seek his aid –
Being needed spoils him, I'm afraid:

123

He suddenly acquires a sense
Of status which breeds insolence.
Still, now those eyes whose dazzling rays
Hold me in thrall are going to blaze
So close to me, I shall declare
My passion to her and lay bare
My very soul... But here they are.
(*Enter TRUFALDIN, MASCARILLE.*)
TRUFALDIN: For once, it seems, a lucky star
Is shining on me! In what way,
What paltry coin, can I repay
The *guardian angel* standing here?
LELIE: (*Putting on a Middle Eastern accent.*) What? Me? An
angel? The idea!
It was a fluke, sir, nothing more.
TRUFALDIN: I'm sure I've seen this man before.
MASCARILLE: He *looks* like somebody you've met –
I told you that – but don't forget:
There aren't that many types of face –
Resemblances are commonplace.
TRUFALDIN: You've seen my son, the only light
In my benighted life?
LELIE: That's right.
He looked well. Very well indeed.
TRUFALDIN: He spoke of me?
LELIE: Do birds eat seed?
He spoke of nothing else.
MASCARILLE: Not *quite.*
LELIE: Your face, your mien, your manner, right
Down to the dimple on your chin.
TRUFALDIN: What? So precise? He can't have been –
He hasn't seen me in ten years.
MASCARILLE: Astonishing though it appears
Parents do linger in the mind –
I can recall my own, I find,
In minute...
TRUFALDIN: (*Sceptical now, to LELIE.*) Which *town* is he in?
LELIE: A town in Turkey... errrrrrrrrrrrrmmmmmmmmm...
Turin.

TRUFALDIN: Turin, you say? That's in Piedmont.
MASCARILLE: (*Aside.*) Oh, God, how *brainless* do you want?
(*To TRUFALDIN.*) *Tunis* – that's where he saw your son –
You heard him wrong. You must have done:
Armenian consonants aren't like ours.
TRUFALDIN: (*Dryly.*) But your interpretative powers
Have saved the day. (*To LELIE.*) He did disclose
My real name to you, I suppose?
MASCARILLE: Giorgio Ruberti, do you mean?
LELIE: That's you, that's who you've always been
Trufaldin's just a soubriquet.
TRUFALDIN: Where was he born?
MASCARILLE: I love the *bay...*
See it and die, or so they say...
Naples – a most enchanting spot! –
Although in your case maybe not.
TRUFALDIN: Did I ask you?
LELIE: Your son's birthplace?
Naples, of course.
TRUFALDIN: I sent Horace
Away at twelve to study – where?
With whom?
MASCARILLE: A good man, that Albert,
They've been together, haven't they,
All through Boulogne, and after?
TRUFALDIN: (*In protest, to MASCARILLE.*) Hey!
MASCARILLE: (*Aside.*) If I can't cut this meeting short
We're dead.
TRUFALDIN: (*To LELIE.*) I want a full report
Give me some details – question one:
This pirate ship that they were they on –
What was its name?
(*He rounds on MASCARILLE, thinking he's about to prompt
LELIE again.*)
MASCARILLE: I've no idea!
I wasn't going to interfere –
That was a yawn. But I suggest
Our friend here gets some food and rest –
He's come so far, it's getting late.

LELIE: Don't worry, I already ate.

MASCARILLE: You'd like a little more, perhaps –
Some bread and cheese? to fill the gaps?

TRUFALDIN: Then be my guest, sir – go in – please.
(*TRUFALDIN motions to LELIE to go into the house.*)

LELIE: You first.

MASCARILLE: The social niceties
Are not observed where he comes from.
(*Reluctantly, TRUFALDIN goes in.*)
Well, what panache, sir, what aplomb!

LELIE: He caught me off guard. Never fear,
I'll be much steadier from here –
Yes, now the real fun can begin.

MASCARILLE: Here comes Léandre. Let's go in.
(*They go. Enter LEANDRE and ANSELME.*)

ANSELME: Great pity, last night's escapade –
People are talking, I'm afraid –
To think a *slave girl's* caught your eye!
I blush for you. You want *her? Why?*
Clearly my honour *is* concerned,
It *is* my daughter that you've spurned
And that's embarrassed me, of course,
But my shame couldn't equal yours.
Please – don't demean yourself – be wise,
Give this girl up, open your eyes –
You've erred. Fine, everybody errs.
But if we make our errors worse
By sticking to them, then, dear boy,
We *are* in trouble. You'll enjoy
This creature for a while – then what?
Will you still love her? I think not.
Your love can follow but one course:
A month of bliss, years of remorse;
Her only dowry is her face,
Beauty's no grounds on which to base
A *marriage!* For a night or two
She will be all in all to you
But when the night's attractions fade

There'll still be *days* through which to wade,
Terrible days – despair, distress,
Anxiety – a total mess –
Your *father* will abandon you
He'll cut you off without a sou –
Lord, what an absolute *nightmare!*
LEANDRE: I know that, sir. I'm well aware
That I am honoured by your choice
And that I really should rejoice
In being loved by one so far
Above my own pathetic star
So pure, so beautiful. What's more...
ANSELME: Somebody's opening that door,
Someone we might not care to meet
Let's slip away, and be discreet.
(*As a servant emerges from the house, they go.*)
(*A blackout suggests the passage of an hour, after which*
MASCARILLE and LELIE come out of TRUFALDIN's house.)
MASCARILLE: The whole plan's all but fallen through
Thanks to the pranks we've had from you.
LELIE: Off again are we? Moan moan moan!
I did all right, I held my own.
MASCARILLE: Oh, your performance was just fine!
You said all Turks were heathen swine
Worshippers of the moon and sun –
Par for the course that, no harm done –
What really put the wind up me
Was your behaviour with Célie:
Couldn't you keep your love in check?
You were a caldron, flipping heck!
A great *tureen* of steaming stew
Stuck on a high flame, that was you,
Just *boiling over* everywhere!
LELIE: Me? Boiling over! That's not fair.
I scarcely even spoke to her.
MASCARILLE: But anybody could infer
From your *behaviour* how things stood,
Your *face* said more than speeches could:

127

MOLIERE

In one meal you gave more away
Than normal lovers would betray
In a whole year.
LELIE: Oh, don't talk rot.
MASCARILLE: The signs you gave off!
LELIE: Such as what?
MASCARILLE: You acted like a silly arse:
    Drinking her wine, out of her glass,
    Not bothering to wipe it clean,
    With your lips where her lips had been;
    Snapping up morsels from her plate
    Which she had tried and you then ate,
    Pounced on, in fact – well, how absurd;
    You blushed; you scarcely said a word;
    You ogled her, without a thought
    About the risk of being caught;
    To make the pantomime complete
    You kept on jiggling with your feet
    Under the table – what a racket!
    When our host could no longer hack it
    He kicked the dog, *two* dogs, poor things –
    They suffered for *your* jigglings!
LELIE: That's right, condemn me out of hand,
    Of course, you wouldn't understand,
    You're not in love. To please you, though,
    I *will* try not to let it show
    And...
    (*TRUFALDIN comes out of the house.*)
MASCARILLE: We were speaking of your son.
TRUFALDIN: A word please.
    (*Draws MASCARILLE to one side.*)
                                        Guess what I've just done.
MASCARILLE: I've no idea. Enlighten me.
TRUFALDIN: I've found a very tough old tree
    And cut a branch off, slim and strong,
    Two inches thick and four feet long,
    Just right, in other words.
MASCARILLE: What for?
TRUFALDIN: Making your back extremely sore.

128

And his, the lying little swine –
How dare he spin that stupid line?
'Merchant' 'Armenian' my eye!
MASCARILLE: You mean you think that was a lie?
TRUFALDIN: Give up. You've nothing left to hide.
I've rumbled you. I *know* you've lied.
He told Célie why you were here –
My daughter happened to be near –
She heard it all. You're in the plot,
You are his henchman.
MASCARILLE: No I'm not.
TRUFALDIN: Prove it. Let's see you drive him out.
Take this and give him a good clout.
(*He hands MASCARILLE the stick.*)
MASCARILLE: Gladly... I'll give him such a thwack –
In fact I'll rearrange his back.
(*Under his breath, to LELIE.*) Sir, now I'm going to
                                    make you pay
For being such a shower all day.
(*TRUFALDIN goes over to LELIE.*)
TRUFALDIN: So: you'd make fools of honest folk?
MASCARILLE: Armenian merchant! What a joke!
Take that, and that.
(*He wallops LELIE with the stick.*)
LELIE: Hang on!
MASCARILLE: And this!
LELIE: You're killing me!
TRUFALDIN: I hope he is!
(*MASCARILLE continues to hit LELIE.*)
Splendid! I feel much better now.
(*TRUFALDIN takes back the stick and goes in.*)
LELIE: Just what was that in aid of? (*Feeling a bruise.*) Ow!
MASCARILLE: Are you all right?
LELIE: Am I all what?!!
MASCARILLE: Couldn't you curb your tongue, you clot?
Don't you know daughters have sharp ears?
So yet again it ends in tears
Thanks to your folly, but this time –

You've paid in bruises for your crime,
I needn't scold you, or get mad
I've let off all the steam I had.
LELIE: Traitor! You're going to pay for this!
MASCARILLE: You're staring into the abyss
And it's your fault.
LELIE: What do you mean?
MASCARILLE: On top moronic form you've been.
LELIE: I have?
MASCARILLE: You gave the game away,
Trufaldin's daughter heard you say
To your beloved why we'd come.
Even by *your* lights that was dumb.
Do you play cards? Avoid piquet.
LELIE: Christ, what a nightmare of a day!
But then to beat me black and blue...
MASCARILLE: He thought that I was in it too.
I had to prove that wasn't so.
LELIE: You hit me with such *venom,* though!
MASCARILLE: I had to make the thing look real.
I won't pretend I didn't feel
A certain *urge* to do it, too –
I mean, it *was* long overdue.
Can we forget it? If we can
I promise you I'm still you're man,
Tomorrow night she will be yours,
But if you're bent on settling scores
I shan't assist you any more.
LELIE: My back's is really *very* sore
But only you can save my cause.
MASCARILLE: There's a non-interference clause...
LELIE: I accept both conditions.
MASCARILLE: Good.
All right, now run along, I would,
And get a poultice for your back.
You promise your resolve won't crack –
You won't throw in your tuppence-worth...?
LELIE: Not for the kingdoms of the earth! (*Goes.*)

MASCARILLE: Back to the drawing board – again,
Racking my poor old worn-out brain.
ERGASTE: Ah, Mascarille, I have some news:
I think if I were in your shoes
I'd be alarmed – your bird has flown
Or nearly – someone's come to town,
A gypsy (though his skin's not brown)
With an old wrinkled crone in tow –
He's quite well-heeled, as gypsies go,
I think he's out to get his paws
On what's her name? that girl of yours.
He's going to buy the luscious bint.
MASCARILLE: Aha – I heard her drop a hint
About a suitor she'd once had –
I'll bet you this is him. Too bad.
I might have known we'd come unstuck
Just when he'd had a stroke of luck:
One minute we are chuffed to learn
That our main reason for concern,
Léandre, has had his chances wrecked –
A visit he did not expect
Put paid to them – out of the blue
His dad appeared and forced him to
Accept a match with Hippolyte;
Now, with him gone, we promptly meet
Another problem just as dire
Real genius this one will require...
I *think* I *can* still save the day:
I'll stop them leaving, that delay
Will give me time, and then, who knows?
I might bring matters to a close.
Suppose I put about a tale
Designed to get him thrown in gaol –
First there's the general attitude
To gypsies – they're not kindly viewed –
Then, this one's rich, which makes it worse
For him, coz lots of officers
Make money by imprisoning

Rich men who've not done anything
Then charging them to set them free –
It's bold, but it might work – we'll see.

End of Act Four.

ACT FIVE

MASCARILLE, ERGASTE.

MASCARILLE is dressed as a secretary, including little round-rimmed spectacles. He has a notice in his right hand.

MASCARILLE: The imbecile! The bungling fool!
    It's torture. It's unjust! It's cruel!
ERGASTE: It looked as though you couldn't fail,
    Not once the gypsy'd gone to jail,
    And then your master bursts in there
    Protesting that 'he cannot bear
    To see a good man treated so!'
    When they refuse to let him go
    He lays about him, if you please,
    Makes minced-meat of the deputies!
MASCARILLE: And so ensures his rival's getting
    The girl *he* wants, the stupid cretin!
ERGASTE: Can't stand here chatting, though, alas –
    Got things to do. (*Goes.*)
MASCARILLE: The stupid *ass!*
    This latest antic is his best!
    Superb! I reckon he's possessed:
    Some Bungle Demon's seized his soul
    And means to drive me up the pole
    By making sure that anywhere
    He can do damage, he'll be there!
    But I can beat that demon yet.
    The game's not over, just one set.
    Célie is far from keen to go,
    She sees it as a dreadful blow
    To leave my master. (*Glancing off.*) Here they come.
    This house here is my home from home
    I even have a set of keys
    I come and go here as I please,
    Let's sow a seed and see what grows –
    But, God, the lengths to which one goes!

(*MASCARILLE pins the notice on the door of the house, then
exits one side, just as CELIE and ANDRES enter the other.*)
ANDRES: Célie, I've done so much to prove
 The depth, the *ardour* of my love:
 At twenty, the Venetians saw
 Stout service from me in the war –
 I could have gained a good post there –
 Then I met you – what did I care
 For posts or honours after that?
 All vistas I rejected, flat,
 Except those that included you –
 I joined your people to pursue
 My goal, with every waking breath
 I followed it: brushes with death,
 Your coldness, nothing could deter
 My steadfast heart, until we were
 Divided by a twist of fate –
 I lost you, but how obdurate
 I've been since then, one end in view
 Through thick and thin: to be with *you*.
 And then I met a gypsy crone
 Who told me how they had been thrown
 Into quite desperate straits, how *you*
 Were sacrificed to pull them through,
 Sold into slavery for gold.
 Now I'm here, waiting to be told
 What is your wish, I've set you free
 Now tell me what you'll do with me!
CELIE: Andrès, you've been so kind, so good,
 I fear my melancholy mood
 Must look like rank ingratitude.
 To one who's rescued me from Hell.
 In my defence, I *am* unwell,
 I have a headache, I'm in pain,
 Let's wait till I'm myself again,
 Then, if we must, we'll board a ship.
ANDRES: By all means let's postpone our trip.
 It was to serve you that I came

Your comfort is my only aim –
Somewhere for you to convalesce,
That's what we want
(*Seeing the house, the notice on the door clearly visible.*)
                    and, at a guess,
We might find all we need in *there.*
(*He goes up to the door and reads the notice, then knocks. The disguised MASCARILLE opens the door.*)
MASCARILLE: Was ist? How can I help, mein herr?
ANDRES: Is this your house?
MASCARILLE: Jawohl, das ist.
I'll serve you, sir, while here du bist.
ANDRES: We're looking for a place to stay.
MASCARILLE: To rrrent a rrroom? Vhy, zo you may.
To peoples of gut charrracter
I let rrrooms. Are you gut? Und her?
ANDRES: This is a house of good repute
I'm sure.
MASCARILLE: Vill von, or two rrrooms suit?
Iz she your schwester or your vife? (*Indicating CELIE.*)
ANDRES: Neither.
MASCARILLE: Zee other? It is rrrife.
ANDRES: She's *not* that *either!* Never mind –
I'll fetch my crone, and then I'll find
A carriage.
MASCARILLE: (*Indicating CELIE.*) Macht sie etwas schrein?
ANDRES: A headache.
MASCARILLE: Zen I give her vine.
Fine vine I have, und also cheese.
(*To CELIE.*) Enter my humble dvelling, please.
(*He ushers CELIE into the house.*
Enter LELIE.)
LELIE: Although my passion's very strong
To interfere now would be wrong.
All I can do is sit and wait,
Just leave things in the hands of fate –
He is in charge, it's been agreed.
(*Seeing ANDRES.*) Sir, is there something here you need?

ANDRES: A room. I've rented one. In there.

LELIE: My father owns it. But it's spare.
Our valet sleeps there every night,
He's the nightwatchman.

ANDRES: Is that right?
The notice just says: 'ROOMS TO LET'.

LELIE: We're not *that* short of money yet!
Who put that notice up? Ah, yes!
Oh Lord! I reckon I can guess.
The valet I just spoke about –
He put it up, without a doubt,
This is his latest *ruse*, I'll bet,
To nab the girl I'm trying to get,
A *gypsy* I've been smitten by.

ANDRES: I couldn't ask her *name*, could I?

LELIE: Célie.

ANDRES: Célie! I wish you'd said.
You could have simply asked, instead
Of going to such lengths. You see:
I've *bought* her, she belongs to me.

LELIE: Good God!

ANDRES: I'm glad you've told me this.

LELIE: Can you revive my hopes of bliss?
Can you...?

ANDRES: I'll sort this out today.

LELIE: I'm speechless! How can I repay...?

ANDRES: No, really, sir, don't bother, please.
(*Enter MASCARILLE.*)

MASCARILLE: (*Seeing LELIE.*) He spreads himself like a
                                        disease.
Now what's he doing, damn his eyes?

LELIE: That *is* a wonderful disguise.
It would have fooled *me*. (*To MASCARILLE.*) Mascarille,
Come here, please.

MASCARILLE: Bitte, wer sind Sie?
Und who is Mascarille, mein herr?
There's no such man zat I'm aware.

LELIE: Oh, very drôle!

THE IDIOT: ACT FIVE

MASCARILLE: You laugh at me?

Aus! Aus! (*Trying to shoo him away.*)

LELIE: Hilarious, isn't he?

(*To MASCARILLE.*) Drop this charade please.

MASCARILLE: Wer bist du?

Aus, aus, before I murder you!

LELIE: This German act's superfluous.

We've worked things out, the two of us.

MASCARILLE: You have?

ANDRES: (*To LELIE.*)   Wait here. I won't be long. (*Goes.*)

LELIE: Impressed?

MASCARILLE: Perhaps I got you wrong.

LELIE: You *had* to keep up your disguise

You couldn't simply recognise

That I'd been useful for a change

MASCARILLE: I would have found it very strange.

I still do.

LELIE: But you must admit

This is a coup, and thanks to it

My earlier slate has been wiped clean?

MASCARILLE: You've had a stroke of luck, you mean.

(*Enter ANDRES and CELIE.*)

ANDRES: Is she the girl, then?

LELIE: This is she.

ANDRES: You've been extremely kind to me

And it's a debt I must repay

With promptitude – but not *this* way,

Not with a creature I adore.

My heart would not survive it, nor

Would you desire it, surely? No,

You're a kind man. I have to go.

Goodbye now, for a day or two.

(*Exit ANDRES.*)

MASCARILLE: Oh, yes indeed, sir – quite a 'coup'.

I've got to laugh... I don't want to.

LELIE: That's it, this *is* the final straw,

You're not to help me any more,

I don't deserve it, I'm a clown,

Whatever *you* build *I* pull down,

137

Constantly queering my own pitch,
Farewell, my friends! I'll find a ditch
And then I'll lie in it face down
Until I freeze to death or drown –
Then I'll be harmless – I'll have died. (*Goes.*)
MASCARILLE: The crowning folly: suicide.
I'm going to let him off, of course,
It's just redeemed him, that remorse,
Besides, I vowed that I would best
The imp by which he is possessed –
My victory will be hard won
But therefore a more glorious one.
CELIE: What can I do? I'm torn apart:
He's set me free, *he's* won my heart!
But my own feelings have no weight –
To have been saved from a dire fate
Is far more binding, in the end:
Andrès can only be a friend,
I'll never pay the debt I owe
By loving him, but, even so,
He has the stronger claim on me –
I can't desert him for Lélie.
We'll both be miserable of course
But duty is a powerful force.
Now: what do you propose to try
Or have you, too, kissed hope goodbye?
MASCARILLE: It's tricky, but, for what it's worth
I shall be moving Heaven and Earth. (*Goes.*)
(*Enter HIPPOLYTE.*)
HIPPOLYTE: Great is the hatred, *and* the fear
You've roused in... certain ladies here
By preying, with your *vast* allure,
On hearts we thought we held secure.
Men seem unable to resist
You add a conquest to your list
Each day, and all at our expense,
Small wonder if we take offence.
If only, in the general rout,
You'd condescend to leave *one* out

Or let me take one back again
I'd see no reason to complain,
But I *have* reason, do I not,
When you just swoop and scoop the lot.
CELIE: I hope you'll exercise restraint,
Not terrorise me with complaint,
That face must give you confidence
Surely you have sufficient sense
Of your *own* beauty not to be
Afraid of challenges from *me.*
HIPPOLYTE: The world knows what I say is true:
That you have managed to subdue
Léandre and Lélie. Your spell
Has worked on other hearts as well –
We'll let them pass.
CELIE: If this is so
It surely can't be such a blow,
Or such a black deed on my part:
Who wants to keep a faithless heart?
HIPPOLYTE: I have no cause for bitterness:
They love you, how can they do less?
Who wouldn't love that form, that face?
It's with no rancour, not a trace,
That I now take Léandre back
Forced by his father to change tack
And marry me.
(*Enter MASCARILLE.*)
MASCARILLE: Amazing news!
Prepare to wonder and enthuse!
CELIE: What is it?
MASCARILLE: Jesus, *what* a day!
It going to end just like a play!
CELIE: *What* is?
MASCARILLE: The crone was in the square,
The gypsy hag, when, from nowhere,
Another, very ancient, weird
And evil-looking hag appeared –
She walked up boldly to the first

139

And peered into her face, and cursed,
She wasn't pleased with what she saw –
At first she simply cursed and swore,
Then she attacked her – it was war!
They had no swords or muskets, though,
But with their nails (the six or so
Old carious claws that they retained)
They tore such flesh as there remained
Off one other's crumbling bones,
These two infuriated crones,
And, oh, the *oaths* on either side:
'Bitch! Gorgon! Filthy slut!' they cried
Their wigs flew off during the fight –
A farcical but frightening sight
They constituted after that –
Two vultures locked in fierce combat
Until, attracted by the din,
Andrès came up with Trufaldin
And prized apart the crazy pair.
Now one of them began to stare
At Trufaldin (this was the one
Whose furious insults had begun
The contretemps) 'Can it be you?
Or am I seeing things? I knew
That you were living in these parts
Under an alias... my heart's
About to burst, my joy's too great,
Just when I thought it was too late,
Giorgio Ruberti! Yes!' (she said)
'When, leaving wife and child, you fled
From Naples, I was nursing there,
You'd placed your daughter in my care,
If you recall – a lovely child,
She would grow up to drive men wild,
As I, for one, already saw
Albeit she was only four.
This woman is a sorceress
Who wormed her way by artfulness

Into our home, and stole the child.
Your wife could not be reconciled
To such a loss, and soon she died.
For my part, I was petrified
Of what you'd say or do – I *mean:*
In *whose* charge had your treasure been?
I sent you word that both were dead –
Let half that tale now be unsaid
And let *her* tell us, for 'tis she,
Just what *has* happened to Célie.'
Out came all that, and *with* it came
A few more mentions of the name
Giorgio Ruberti. Hearing it
Andrès's features had been lit
By what I'd call a *mounting glow.*
'Joseph and Mary! GIORGIO!'
He now exclaimed, 'the man I've sought
For years, in vain, or so I thought –
Have I been looking at your face
And failed to know you? I'm Horace!
Your son! After I lost Albert,
Discovering interests elsewhere,
I left Boulogne, and study, for
A wandering life, in which I saw
Much of the world. Six years flew past
Before my wild thoughts turned at last
To home, and to my family,
Which, suddenly, I longed to see.
I went to Naples, scoured the place,
Of you, though, I could find no trace,
No, nothing did I see or hear
Save a few rumours, all unclear;
One I decided to pursue
To Venice – where I found no clue
As to your whereabouts. Since then
I've drawn a blank, time and again,
You'd changed your name, that's all I knew.'
Whether or not this story blew

Trufaldin higher than the skies
I leave you ladies to surmise.
(*To CELIE.*) He has acknowledged you; Andrès
Is now your brother, and unless
They introduce some strange new law
He'll have to give you up. Therefore,
Because he seems to owe some debt
To my young master, he's now set
On seeing you and Lélie wed.
Lélie's old man's already said
That just for once he doesn't mind,
And, lest the joy should be confined,
His daughter is to wed Horace.
Well, there you are: in one hour's space
These miracles have all occurred.
CELIE: I caught my breath at every word.
MASCARILLE: The hags are worn out from their row,
The rest are on their way right now.
Léandre, (*To HIPPOLYTE.*) your father – everyone.
I must report how things have gone
To You-know-who, and let him know
That in his hour of deepest woe
Just when his plight could get no graver
Fate has decided in his favour. (*Goes.*)
(*Enter TRUFALDIN, ANDRES, ANSELME, PANDOLFE,
LEANDRE.*)
CELIE: Father!
TRUFALDIN: You've heard?
CELIE: What wondrous news!
HIPPOLYTE: (*To LEANDRE.*) Some crimes there's no need
                                      to excuse,
And one such, surely, must be yours,
Now that I've seen its Heavenly cause.
LEANDRE: Before I ask it, you forgive!
One thing I swear, though, as I live:
When father made me take your hand
He *forced* what I'd already *planned*.
ANDRES: (*To CELIE.*) To think that Nature should have
                                      banned

A love so innocent and pure!
My conduct does at least ensure
That with no change, or very slight,
Its flame may burn on, just as bright!
CELIE: And while my own flame feebly burned
I wished your love could be returned
I blamed my coldness. Now I find
Behind it all a sense of *kind,*
An *instinct,* making me step back
From such a sweet, but slippery track!
TRUFALDIN: I find you, and, in the same day,
I give you summarily away!
Some father I turned out to be!
CELIE: Your wish, sir, is my destiny.
(*Enter MASCARILLE and LELIE.*)
MASCARILLE: No danger from your evil sprite,
Not now, sir – it's all watertight,
It's all so straight now, even you
Could scarcely make it go askew,
Or drop her with your clumsy paws:
Fate's beaten you, Célie is yours.
LELIE: Has Heaven finally decreed
That I should be...
TRUFALDIN: It has indeed,
No doubt of it... *dear* son-in-law!
PANDOLFE: It's done! It's in the bag!
ANDRES: What's more
I've paid my debt.
LELIE: Well, in that case
There's somebody I must embrace
Embrace a thousand times... (*To MASCARILLE.*)
Come here!
(*When MASCARILLE doesn't go to him, LELIE grabs him
and hugs him tightly.*)
MASCARILLE: Hey! Hang on! What's the big idea?
You've taken all my breath away
And that was just for your valet –
(*To CELIE.*) God knows what maulings are in store
For *you!*

TRUFALDIN: (*To LEANDRE.*) Your father's been sent for –
My dear friends, here's what I propose:
Let's bring this great day to a close
Together, since so much distress
Has ended, and such happiness
Begun today.
MASCARILLE: You're all well set.
But no one's thought about *me* yet.
Don't *I* get anybody's hand?
I look at all this coupling, and
It seems a game I'd like to play.
ANSELME: I'll fix it.
MASCARILLE: What more need I say?
Except: let Heaven answer the men's prayers
And send them babies who are really theirs.

The End.

Printed in the USA
CPSIA information can be obtained
at www.ICGtesting.com
LVHW020953171024
794056LV00004B/1101